Advance Praise for Amy James's Knowledge Esse

"Knowledge Essentials is a remarkable series that will benefit children of all abilities and learning styles. Amy James has taken a close look at curriculum standards and testing around the country and developed simple and creative activities that support what's being taught at each grade level, while remaining sensitive to the fact that children learn at different rates and in different ways. I highly recommend it for all parents who want to make a difference in their children's education."

—Michael Gurian, author of *Boys and Girls Learn Differently* and *The Wonder of Boys*

"Finally, a book about teaching young children by somebody who knows her stuff! I can (and will) wholeheartedly recommend this series to the ever-growing number of parents who ask me for advice about how they can help their children succeed in elementary school."

—LouAnne Johnson, author of *Dangerous Minds* and *The Queen of Education*

"Having examined state standards nationwide, Amy James has created innovative and unique games and exercises to help children absorb what they *have* to learn, in ways that will help them *want* to learn. Individualized to the child's own learning style, this is a must-have series for parents who want to maximize their child's ability to succeed in and out of the classroom."

—Myrna B. Shure, Ph.D., author of *Thinking Parents, Thinking Child*

"The books in Amy James's timely and unique Knowledge Essentials series give parents a clear idea of what their children are learning and provide the tools they need to help their children live up to their full academic potential. This is must reading for any parent with a school-age child."

—Michele Borba, Ed.
Everybody Hate

SECOND GRADE SUCCESS

KNOWLEDGE
ESSENTIALS™

SECOND GRADE SUCCESS

Everything You Need to Know
to Help Your Child Learn

AMY JAMES

JOSSEY-BASS
A Wiley Imprint
www.josseybass.com

Published by Jossey-Bass
A Wiley Imprint
989 Market Street, San Francisco, CA 94103-1741

Design and composition by Navta Associates, Inc.

Jossey-Bass books and products are available through most bookstores. To contact Jossey-Bass directly call our Customer Care Department within the U.S. at 800-956-7739, outside the U.S. at 317-572-3986, or fax 317-572-4002.

Jossey-Bass also publishes its books in a variety of electronic formats. Some content that appears in print may not be available in electronic books.

Library of Congress Cataloging-in-Publication Data:

James, Amy, date.
   Second grade success : everything you need to know to help your child learn / Amy James.
      p. cm.
   Includes bibliographical references and index.
   ISBN-13 978-0-471-46820-2 (pbk.)
   ISBN-10 0-471-46820-7 (pbk.)
  1. Second grade (Education) 2. Second grade (Education)—Curricula—United States.
3. Education, Elementary—Parent participation.   I. Title.
   LB15712nd .J36 2005
   372.24'1—dc22   2004022625

Printed in the United States of America

FIRST EDITION
PB Printing 10 9 8 7 6 5 4 3 2 1

To my mother, Cindy King.

CONTENTS

Contents

ACKNOWLEDGMENTS

I would like to thank the following people for advising me on this book:

My mother, Cindy King, is a retired early childhood and reading specialist who taught kindergarten and first grade for thirty years. She assisted in establishing the transition program at her school district for children who are developmentally young.

My father, E. W. James, was an elementary school principal and elementary school teacher for fifteen years. He led the school district's efforts to serve children with special needs.

Gloria Hamlin, my supervising administrator during my teaching years, retired from Norman Public School after spending twenty-two years teaching math and eleven years as a middle school administrator. She directed the math, science, and technology departments.

Elizabeth Hecox is in her sixteenth year of teaching at Kennedy Elementary School in Norman, Oklahoma. She is an incredible classroom teacher, and the book is better because of her work with me on it.

Kim Lindsay is in her twelfth year of teaching elementary school in Dallas Public Schools and in Norman Public Schools. She was elected teacher of the year at Kennedy Elementary School for 2001–2002.

Holly Sharp taught English language arts for thirty years in five states and served as department chair for twelve years. She has written curriculum for Norman Public Schools and is an advisory board member for both the University of Oklahoma and Norman Public Schools.

The employees of Six Things, Inc., are a group of more than twenty current and former teachers who provide invaluable assistance on a daily basis. Anytime I needed help in any subject area, for any grade, their enormously good brains were at my disposal. This book series would not be possible without their assistance, and I am eternally grateful to them for their help.

Introduction

Congratulations! You made it through a whole year of sack lunches, field trips, homework folders, and handouts. Now it's time to get geared up for second grade.

Second grade may not seem nearly as new and exciting as kindergarten and first grade, but it is—and it may be even more so. You and your child already know the routine, and there is something to be said for routines. Your child knows that school isn't scary at all and that it can be really fun. Learning starts to take a faster pace because your child is a reader now. It is a lot easier to learn (and to teach) many new things when children can read. This is the time when you start to get amazed at what your child knows.

The second grade year is pivotal because your child's learning personality and patterns are beginning to emerge and are still malleable. Home, your child's first learning environment, is the primary testing ground for new knowledge and skill sets. Home also sets the tone, or pattern, for learning. If you set reasonable expectations and help your child establish consistent learning patterns, you will both enjoy the stability and advancement it brings to your child's academic life.

Life at home matters as much now as it ever did. If you want to raise a thinking child, you need to give him or her many opportunities to think. Speak in complete sentences at home. Articulate thoughts to your child about everyday things as well as abstract concepts by talking and laughing. Bringing the level of content and conversation in your daily life to the one that is in your child's school life doesn't have to be boring or burdensome.

Getting the Most from This Book

This book is a guide to creating an exceptional learning environment in your home. It contains curricula and skills unique to second grade presented in a way that makes it easy to put what you learn into practice immediately. This book serves as a tool to help solve the mystery behind creating a supportive, learning-rich environment in your home that fosters a thinking child's development while enriching her curricula. It contains dozens of mini–lesson plans that contain easy-to-use activities designed to help your child meet your state's learning requirements. An environmental learning section in each chapter tells you how to identify learning opportunities in the everyday world.

Chapters 2 through 4 give you some child development information to get you started. Teaching is about knowing the subject area you teach, but moreover it is about knowing the abilities of the students you teach. As a parent you can easily see the milestones your child reaches at an early age (crawling, walking, talking, etc.), but milestones are not always apparent in your six- to nine-year-old. These chapters explain the child development processes that take place during second grade, including what thinking milestones your child's brain is capable of and will reach in normal development during this time. In order for you to teach effectively, you will need to account for these developmental milestones in all topics and skills that you introduce.

Teaching is also about recognizing how different people learn and tailoring the way you teach to suit them. You will find out how to recognize different learning styles in chapter 3, which will help you implement the learning activities in the rest of the book.

Chapters 5 through 10 provide general subject area information for the second grade curriculum. The curriculum discussed in this book was chosen by reviewing all fifty of the state learning standards, the National Subject Area Association learning standards, the core curriculum materials that many school districts use, and supplemental education products. While there are some discrepancies in curricula from region to region, they are few and far between. Chances are that even if you aren't able to use all of the topical subject area units (such as social studies and science), you will be able to use most of them. Reading, writing, and math are skill-based subjects, particularly in second grade, and those skills are chosen according to specific child developmental indicators. It is likely that you will be able to use all of the information in those chapters. Each chapter provides learning activities that you can do at home with your child.

The focus of chapter 12 is understanding the social environment in second grade, including how your child interacts with peers and his or her social needs. Chapter 13 discusses how your child will demonstrate that he or she is prepared for third grade. The appendixes provide information on products that meet certain second grade learning needs.

You won't read this book from cover to cover while lounging on the beach. Hopefully it will be a raggedy, dog-eared, marked-up book that has been thumbed through, spilled on, and referred to throughout the school year. Here are some tips on using this book:

Do

- Use this book as a reference guide throughout your child's second grade year.

- Model activities and approaches after the information you find in this book when creating your own supplemental learning activities.

- Modify the information to meet your needs and your child's needs.

DON'T

- Complete the activities in this book from beginning to end. Instead, mix and match them appropriately to the curriculum and/or skills your child is learning in school.

- Use this book as a homeschool curriculum. It will help with your homeschooling in the same way it helps parents that don't homeschool—it supplements the second grade core curriculum.

- Challenge your child's teacher based on information you find here. ("Why isn't my child covering ocean life as it said in *Second Grade Success*?") Instead, look for the synergy in the information from both sources.

Use this book and its resources as supplemental information to enhance your child's second grade curriculum—and let's make it a good year for everyone!

Getting the Most for Your Second Grader

1

No parent says, "Oh, mediocre is okay for my child. Please do things halfway; it doesn't matter." Parents want the best for their children. This is not a matter of spending the most money on education or buying the latest educational toy. It is a matter of spending time with your child and expending effort to maximize what he or she is being provided by the school, by the community, and at home.

Getting the Most from Your School System

You wouldn't think twice about getting the most bang for your buck from a hotel, your gym, or a restaurant, and you shouldn't think twice about getting the most from your school system. The school system was designed to serve your needs, and you should take advantage of that.

Public Schools

Part of learning how to manage life as an adult is knowing how to manage interaction with bureaucratic agencies, so it makes sense that part of this learning take place within a kinder, gentler bureaucratic system. This is a good introduction to working within a system that was formed to assist in the development of children's abilities. Schools are also a workplace—with a chain of command—and that is a good induction into the workplace your child will enter as an adult. To further your children's educational experience, you and your children will have the opportunity to meet and work with:

- School personnel: your child's teacher, teacher's aides, specialists, the school counselor, the administrator or principal, and others

- Extracurricular groups: scouts, sports, after-school programs, and community parks and recreation programs

- Parents: of children from your child's class or grade level, school volunteers, and parent–teacher organizations

Participation in your child's education is paramount to his or her success. Active participation doesn't mean that you have to spend hours at the school as a volunteer, but it does include reading all of the communications your school sends either to you directly or home with your child. Also, read the school handbook and drop by your child's school on a regular basis if possible. If you can't stop by, check out the school or class Web site to see what units are being covered, any upcoming events, and so on. Participation means attending school events when you can, going to class parties when possible, and going to parent–teacher conferences. If they are scheduled at a time when you are not available, request a different time. The school administrator or principal usually requires that teachers try to accommodate your schedule.

The single most important thing you can do to get the most out of your local school system is to talk to your child's teacher. Find out what curricula your child will be covering and how you can help facilitate learning. Does the teacher see specific strengths and weaknesses that you can help enhance or bring up to speed? The teacher can help you identify your child's learning style, social skills, problem-solving abilities, and coping mechanisms.

Teachers play a role that extends outside the classroom. Your child's teacher is the perfect person to recommend systemwide and community resources. Teachers know how to find the local scout leaders, tutors, good summer programs, and community resources. Your child's teacher may be able to steer you in the right direction for getting your child on an intramural team. Teachers are truly partners in your child's upbringing.

Your child's teacher cares about your child's well-being. Everyone has heard stories about having a bad teacher or one who was "out to get my child." If that's the way you feel, then it's even more important to have regular conversations with the teacher. Maybe his or her actions or your child's actions are being misunderstood. In any case, your child's teacher is the main source of information about school and the gateway to resources for the year, so find a way to communicate.

If you know there is a problem with the teacher that needs to be taken seriously, try the following:

- Talk to parents with children in the class ahead of your child. They may be able to tell you how the issue was approached by parents the previous year—and they will have lots to tell about their experiences with teachers your child will have next year.

- Talk to your child's principal. This may result in your child being transferred to another class, so make sure you are prepared for that prior to making the appointment. Be willing to work with your child's current teacher prior to transferring your child. The less disruption your second grader experiences, the better.

- Talk to your local school administration center to see what the procedures are for transferring to another school. You will likely be required to provide transportation to a school outside of your home district, but if the problem is severe enough, it will be worth it.

No matter what, active participation and communication with your child's school is essential. It empowers you to:

- Accurately monitor your child's progress

- Determine which optional activities would enrich your child's learning experience

- Prepare your child for upcoming events, curricula, and skill introduction

- Share and add to the school learning environment

- Create a complementary learning environment in your home

- Spend time with your child

And just a word about the school secretary: this person knows more about what is going on in that building than anyone else. When I was a teacher, the school secretary always added to my and my students' success. The secretary is a taskmaster, nurse, mom or dad, and generally just a comforting figure in what can sometimes be a really big building. The school secretary always knows what forms to fill out, which teacher is where, what students are absent and why, when the next school event is, and how much candy money you owe for the latest fund-raiser. He or she is a source of lunch money, milk money, extra pencils, bus passes, and the copy machine. Get to know and love your school secretary.

Private Schools

On a micro level, participating in your child's education if she attends a private school isn't much different from participating if she attends a public school. Private schools have access to the same community resources. If you have a special needs child, the private school should work with local education agencies to see that your child gets the appropriate services. Through active communication and participation, you will derive the same benefits as parents whose children attend public school.

On a macro level, private schools are different from public schools. Private schools are governed not by a school board but by an internal system. This can be both easier and harder to navigate. Dealing with private schools is easier because the schools realize that you are paying tuition every month, so frankly they want to please their customers. Dealing with private schools is harder because they aren't accountable to the community for their actions nor are they governed by the same due processes as the public school system. Check out the school's administration hierarchy to see how decisions are made and what roles have been created for parent governance. Also, get to know the school's secretary.

To really be on top of things, it's a good idea to print a copy of your state's learning standards (see chapter 4) and familiarize yourself with the topics and skills that your state thinks second graders should learn. You can find a copy at www.knowledgeessentials.com. Compare the standards to those of your private school's second grade curriculum. If the curriculum is drastically different from the required state learning standards, your child will have difficulty passing the required state assessments. If your child's curriculum meets and exceeds the standards, your child will be well served by that school.

Private schools have the flexibility to incorporate religious elements or varied teaching philosophies that public schools can't provide. They are not subject to the separation of church and state requirements. Private schools operate without depending on community support (such as bond proposals); so as long as their tuition-paying constituency approves of their methods and the students who graduate from the programs demonstrate success, private schools can implement teaching methods at will that fall out of the mainstream.

Getting the Most from Your Homeschool Curriculum

A little power is a dangerous thing. You are homeschooling your child because you want more control over what and how your child learns and the environment in which he learns it. That is admirable, but don't be fooled. To a large extent, your child's natural ability to learn certain things at certain times will dictate the way you should approach any homeschool curriculum (chapters 2 and 3 explain this more fully). The best thing you can do when starting to homeschool your child is look at books on child development. Start with these:

- *Children's Strategies: Contemporary Views of Cognitive Development*, edited by David F. Bjorklund. Hillsdale, N.J.: Erlbaum Associates, 1990.

- *Piaget's Theory: Prospects and Possibilities*, edited by Harry Beilin. Hillsdale, N.J.: Erlbaum Associates, 1992.

- *Instructional Theories in Action: Lessons Illustrating Selected Theories and Models*, edited by Charles M. Reigeluth. Hillsdale, N.J.: Erlbaum Associates, 1987.

- *All Our Children Learning*, Benjamin S. Bloom. New York: McGraw-Hill, 1981.

You don't have to homeschool your child all by yourself or by limiting yourself to a particular homeschool organization's materials. Each state has some form of a regional education system with centers open to the public. At your public school system's curriculum resource center, you can check out curriculum materials and supplemental materials. Most of these centers have a workroom with things like a die press that cuts out letters and shapes from squares to animals to holiday items. Regional education centers often provide continuing education for teachers, so they usually have some training materials on hand. Look for information about your regional center on your state department of education's Web site. You can find a link to your state department of education at www.knowledgeessentials.com.

You can purchase homeschool curriculum kits designed to provide your child with a lion's share of the materials needed to complete a grade level. You can also buy subject area–specific curricula. It is important to ask the company that sells the curricula to correlate the materials with your state's learning standards so that you can see which standards you need to reinforce with additional activities. You can find the companies that sell these kits at www. knowledgeessentials.com.

Using Supplemental Materials

You cannot expect any single curriculum in any public school, private school, or homeschool to meet all of the learning standards for the grade level and subject area in your state. Many will meet 90 percent of the standards and some will meet 75 percent, which is why there are supplemental materials. Schools use them and so should you. They are simply extra materials that help your child learn more. Examples of these materials include:

- Trade books. These are just books that are not textbooks or work-books—in other words, the kinds of books, fiction and nonfiction, that you would check out at the library or that your child would choose at a bookstore. Trade books don't have to tell about many things in a limited number of pages so they can tell a lot more about a single topic than a textbook can. They give your child a chance to practice skills that she is learning. If you choose wisely, you can find books that use newly learned reading skills, such as compound words, blends, prefixes and suffixes, or rhyming. Sometimes these skills will be set in the context of newly learned science or social studies topics, such as weather, habitats, or your community. Many companies provide these types of books for sale, but the most recognizable one may be Scholastic, Inc. Appendix A lists some books that are really good for second graders.

- Software and the Internet. Schools choose electronic activities and content, such as educational software and Internet sites, and electronic components, such as Leapfrog's LeapMat, allowing your child to expand his content knowledge while implementing skills just learned. Supplementing what your child is learning at school with these resources helps him gain technology skills within a familiar context. If you choose wisely, such as starting with the software choices listed in appendix B of this book, you can sometimes enhance reading skills and/or supplement a social studies or science topic while your child learns to operate a computer—talk about bang for your buck.

- Other materials. Videos, photographs, audio recordings, newspapers—just about anything you can find that helps expand what your child is learning is a supplemental resource. Loosely defined, supplemental resources can include a wide array of materials; your newly trained eye is limited only to what you now know is appropriate for your child.

Now you know what we need to cover, so let's get to it.

Second Grade Development

2

The journey begins. Good teachers base their activities on the developmental stages at which their students are performing. What is a developmental stage and why is it important?

The ability to learn is always related to your child's stage of intellectual development. Developmental stages describe how a child thinks and learns in different growth periods. These periods are loosely defined by age but are more accurately defined by behavior. They are important because children cannot learn something until physical growth gives them certain abilities; children who are at a certain stage cannot be taught the concepts of a higher stage (Brainerd, 1978).

The theory of child development that is the basis for modern teaching was formed by Jean Piaget, who was born in 1896 in Neuchâtel, Switzerland, and died in 1980. His theories have been expanded by other educators but stand as the foundation of today's classroom.

Piaget's Stages of Cognitive Development

Piaget is best known for his stages of cognitive development. He discovered that children think and reason differently at different periods in their lives, and he believed that everyone passes through a sequence of four distinct stages in exactly the same order, but the times in which children pass through them can vary by years. Piaget also described two processes that people use from infancy through adulthood to adapt: assimilation and accommodation. *Assimilation* is the process of using the environment to place information in a category of things you know. *Accommodation* is the process of using the environment to add a new category of things you know. Both tools are implemented throughout life and can be used together to understand a new piece of information.

Okay, did you assimilate and accommodate that? The main thing Piaget tells us is that that kids really can't learn certain information and skills until they reach a certain place in their growth that is determined by years and behaviors. Understanding Piaget's stages is like getting the key to Learning City because it is a behavior map that tells you what your kids are ready to learn. Let's define the stages, then look at the behaviors. Piaget's four stages of cognitive development are:

1. *Sensorimotor stage (0 to 4 years):* In this period, intelligence is demonstrated through activity without the use of symbols (letters and numbers). Knowledge of the world is limited because it is based on actual experiences or physical interactions. Physical development (mobility) allows children to cultivate new intellectual abilities. Children will start to recognize some letters and numbers toward the end of this stage.

2. *Preoperational stage (4 to 7 years):* Intelligence is demonstrated through the use of oral language as well as letters and numbers. Memory is strengthened and imagination is developed. Children don't yet think logically very often, and it is hard for them to reverse their thinking on their own. Your little angel is still pretty egocentric at this age, and that is normal.

3. *Concrete operational stage (7 to 11 years):* As children enter this stage, they begin to think logically and will start to reverse

thinking on their own—for example, they will begin to complete inverse math operations (checking addition with subtraction, etc.). Expressing themselves by writing becomes easier. Logical thinking and expression is almost always about a concrete object, not an idea. Finally, children begin to think about other people more—they realize that things happen that affect others either more or less than they affect themselves.

4. *Formal operational stage (11 years and up):* As children become formally operational, they are able to do all of the things in the concrete operational stage—but this time with ideas. Children are ready to understand concepts and to study scientific theories instead of scientific discoveries. They can learn algebra and other math concepts not represented by concrete objects that can be counted. Whereas every stage until now has continuously moved forward, this is the only stage where a step back occurs. As a teenager, your child will become egocentric once again. It won't be easy for you. Thinking and acting as if the world exists exclusively for him or her is cute behavior for a five-year-old; it is rarely cute for a teenager.

Unfortunately, only 35 percent of high school graduates in industrialized countries obtain formal operations; many people will not ever think formally. However, most children can be taught formal operations.

The graph on page 16 puts the stages in a clear perspective.

Developmental Goals for Seven-Year-Olds and Eight-Year-Olds

Now that you know the basics of developmental indicators, let's get down to the nitty-gritty of what can be expected from your second grader.

Seven- and eight-year-old children are in a stage of development often called middle childhood. They learn rapidly in school and enjoy

Percentage of Students in Piagetian Stages

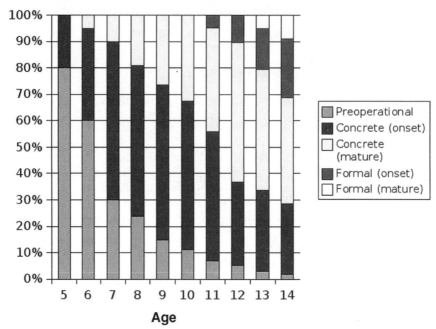

mastering lots of new physical skills. The opinions of their classmates matter more than ever, and they begin to feel the effects of peer pressure.

You will notice physical development changes in your child at this stage, including:

- Large muscles in arms and legs are more developed than small muscles. Children can bounce a ball and run, but it is difficult to do both at the same time.

- There may be quite a difference in the size and abilities of children. This will affect the way they get along with others, how they feel about themselves, and what they do. Seven- to nine-year-old children are learning to use their small muscle skills (printing with a pencil) and their large muscle skills (catching a fly ball).

- Even though children are tired, they may not want to rest. You will need to plan time for them to rest.

A seven-year-old can/will:

- Enjoy testing his or her own strength and skills

- Balance well

- Catch small balls

- Tie shoelaces

- Print his or her full name

- Reverse letters (*b* becomes a *d*)

- Plan and build objects and do crafts

- Read often

- Identify the difference between left and right

- Know the days of the week

- Want to spend a lot of time with friends

- Enjoy rules, rituals, and routines

- Be interested in doing things correctly

- Begin to understand others' views

- View life in absolutes

- Enjoy being around younger children

- Expect to have accomplishments acknowledged

An eight-year-old can/will:

- Manipulate small tools well

- Enjoy testing his or her own strength and skills

- Have good balance

- Be able to catch smaller balls

- Enjoy planning and building activities

- Read often

- Want to be with friends often

- Enjoy rules, rituals, and routines

- Choose same-gender friends more often than not

- Understand others' views (but is still focused primarily on self)

- Enjoy being around younger children

- Wants to do things correctly

Second graders have an increased ability to remember and pay attention, so their ability to speak and express ideas can grow rapidly. Things tend to be black or white, right or wrong, appealing or disgusting, fun or boring to them. There is very little middle ground.

Second graders are able to think and reason more effectively than first graders so they enjoy different types of activities, such as clubs, games with rules, and collecting things. They are learning to plan ahead and evaluate what they do. When you suggest something, don't be surprised if they say, "That's dumb," or, "I don't want to do it."

Second graders are still very self-centered, although they are beginning to think of others. They often say, "That's not fair!" Often, they do not accept rules that they did not help make.

Remember that two children of the same age may be at different stages of development. Every child is an individual with different strengths and weaknesses. Each child needs to feel special and cared about.

Review the rules and limits with your child and let him or her help set them. Change them together when necessary to fit changing situations. Let your child help plan some activities as well as solve some of his or her own problems.

Seven- and eight-year-old children need adults who care about them and will talk and play with them. These are exciting years for the children and for you. You can help them prepare to be healthy teens and adults.

Understanding this stage in a child's development will help you:

- Plan activities to help children be more independent and have fun

- Feel good about what you do as a provider

- Help children be successful and feel good about themselves

Second Grade Learning 3

If you write it on the chalkboard, they will learn it. Sound familiar? If you are lucky, it doesn't—but for a great majority of people it is exactly how they were taught and were expected to learn. Luckily, in most schools, education has come to embrace children with different learning styles.

Learning Styles

Learning styles define how your child learns and processes information. Education experts have identified three main types of learning: visual, auditory, and physical. When learning a new math concept, for example, a visual learner will grasp the material more quickly by reading about it in a book or watching his or her teacher solve a problem on the blackboard. An auditory learner will understand the concept if she can listen to the teacher explain it and then answer questions. A physical learner (also known as tactile-kinesthetic) may need to use blocks, an abacus, or other counting materials (also known as manipulatives) to practice the new concept.

If you understand that your child is a visual learner most of the time—that is, he is most comfortable using sight to explore the world—you can play to his strength and incorporate physical and auditory learning styles when appropriate. It isn't unusual to interchange learning styles for different subjects. An auditory learner can easily use kinesthetic strategies to comprehend new math concepts.

Studies have shown that accommodating a child's learning style can significantly increase his performance at school. In 1992, the U.S. Department of Education found that teaching to a child's learning style was one of the few strategies that improved the scores of special education students on national tests. Identifying your child's learning styles and helping him within that context may be the single most significant factor in his academic achievement. Each activity in the subject area chapters of this book lists variations that help you tailor the activity to your child's learning style. Look for the symbols by the name of each learning style and use these styles to tailor the activities to your child's needs.

Learning styles are pretty easy to spot. All you have to do is watch your child's behavior when given a new piece of information.

👁 Visual

Would you give your right arm to get your child to listen to you? Are your walls a mural comprising every crayon your child has held? If you answered yes, you have a visual learner. You may not be able to get your child to follow two-step oral directions, but she can probably comprehend complex instructions when they are written on the blackboard or listed. Diagrams and graphs are a breeze. Your child can retell complex stories just by looking at one or two pictures from a book. Why is your child seemingly brilliant on paper but a space case when listening? Visual learners rely primarily on their sense of sight to take in information, understand it, and remember it. As long as they can see it, they can comprehend it.

Technically there are two kinds of visual learners: picture learners and print learners. Most children are a mixture of both, although some are one or the other (Willis and Hodson, 1999). Picture learners think in images; if you ask them what sound "oy" makes, they will likely think of a picture of a boy or a toy to remember the sounds of the letters. These kids like to draw—but you knew that by looking at your walls, right? Print learners think in language symbols: letters, numbers, and words. They would think of the actual letters "oy" to remember the sound they make together. Print learners learn to read quickly and are good spellers right off the bat. They also like to write.

Auditory

Is your child a talker? Is total silence the kiss of death to her concentration? Auditory learners understand new ideas and concepts best when they hear and talk about the information. If you observe a group of kids, auditory learners are the ones who learn a tune in a snap just from hearing someone sing it, or who can follow directions to the letter after being told only once or twice what to do. Some auditory learners concentrate better on a task when they have music or noise in the background, or retain new information more accurately when they talk it out. If you ask auditory learners what sound "oy" makes, they will recall the sound first and as many words as possible with that sound almost automatically.

Kinesthetic

Does your child need to touch everything? Physical learners (also known as tactual-kinesthetic learners—*tactual* for touch, *kinesthetic* for movement) use their hands or bodies to absorb new information. In some ways, everyone is a physical learner. If you peek into a classroom, you will see the physical learner tapping a pencil, a finger, or a foot, or twirling her hair to help her concentrate. These kids can't sit still and they are in the top percentile for being diagnosed with attention deficit disorder (ADD).

Before you run to the doctor because your child can't sit still, carefully observe him over a long period of time. Is the movement productive? Does he absorb or block information when moving? If he prefers to feel things in his hands or performs steady movement when trying to concentrate, he is engaging in productive learning.

Physical learners enjoy hands-on activities, such as cutting construction paper, sorting objects with their hands, and building elaborate projects. When you ask physical learners what sound "oy" makes, they will think of the physical cues used by the teacher or the cues they used when learning, such as tapping, physically picking the letters out of the alphabet, or holding *o* and *y* blocks.

Cognitive Learning

Cognitive learning levels are another way that teachers describe how a child processes information. I hear you asking, "Wow, how much of this do I have to remember?"—and you know I am going to say all of it, but it is really important. Let's recap for a minute to see how all of this fits together.

First, you learned about developmental stages, the physical growth that needs to happen before your child can learn certain things. Second, you learned about learning styles, the way your child prefers to process information. Third, you are about to learn about cognitive learning levels, the levels at which your child knows, understands, and can use information that he or she learns. Piaget identified the developmental stages in the 1930s and 1940s. By the 1950s, a group of researchers got together, led by Benjamin Bloom, and created the cognitive learning taxonomy designed to help you understand the levels of learning that can occur with new information. Bloom is often considered one of the most important educational theorists of the twentieth century. He was a professor at the University of Chicago who was more than a brilliant teacher: he was a brilliant thinker. Bloom spent his career researching how thinking and learning happened in students of all ages. Bloom and his researchers broke down the learning levels as follows:

Level 1: Knowledge. The things you know—bits of information that you can memorize, such as the ABCs.

Level 2: Comprehension. The things you understand—knowing the ABCs and understanding that they represent sounds.

Level 3: Application. The things you can apply—knowing the ABCs, understanding that they represent sounds, and then sounding out a word.

Level 4: Analysis. The things you understand well enough to think about them in a new way—knowing the ABCs, understanding that they represent sounds, sounding out a word, and then figuring out what the word means.

Level 5: Synthesis. Understanding something well enough to apply it to a new situation—knowing the ABCs, understanding that they represent sounds, sounding out a word, figuring out what the word means, and using it in a new way.

Level 6: Evaluation. Understanding something so well that you can tell if it is being used correctly—knowing the ABCs, understanding that they represent sounds, sounding out a word, figuring out what the word means, using it in a new way, and then figuring out if the new way is right.

Check the Bloom's Cognitive Learning Levels table on page 26 for some specific key words and behaviors for each level. Getting to know the key words will help you determine how to ask your child questions in order to find out the level at which your child understands new information. Use the examples in the right-hand column of the table to ask questions that check for each level of understanding.

Bloom's Cognitive Learning Levels

Cognitive Level	Verb	Key Words		Examples
Knowledge Recalls data. Exhibits memory of previously learned material by recalling facts and basic concepts.	Remember	choose define describe find how identify knows label list match name omit outline recall	recognize reproduce select show spell state tell what when where which who why	• Defines terminology/vocabulary • Describes details and elements • Recognizes classifications and categories • Knows principles, generalizations, theories, models, and structures • Knows subject-specific skills, algorithms, techniques, and methods • Names criteria for using certain procedures • Spells words • Outlines facts, events, stories, or ideas
Comprehension Demonstrates understanding of facts and ideas by organizing, comparing, translating, interpreting, giving descriptions, and stating main ideas. Understands the meaning, translation, interpolation, and interpretation of instructions and problems.	Understand	classify compare comprehend contrast convert defend demonstrate distinguish estimate explain extend illustrate	infer interpret outline paraphrase predict relate rephrase rewrite show summarize translate	• Summarizes or retells information • Translates an equation • Outlines the main ideas • Summarizes instructions, facts, details, or other things • Compares and contrasts ideas • Explains what is happening • Identifies statements to support a conclusion • Classifies information

Bloom's Cognitive Learning Levels

Cognitive Level	Verb	Key Words		Examples
Application Solves problems in new situations by applying acquired knowledge, facts, techniques, and rules in a different way. Uses a concept in a new situation or unprompted use of an abstraction. Applies what was learned in the classroom into novel situations.	Apply	apply build change choose compute construct demonstrate develop discover identify interview manipulate	model modify operate plan predict prepare produce relate select show solve utilize	• Applies a formula to solve a problem • Uses a manual to solve a problem • Describes how to use something • Finds examples to help apply ideas, rules, steps, or an order • Describes a result • Modifies ideas, rules, steps, or an order for use in another way • Selects facts to demonstrate something
Analysis Examines and breaks information into parts by identifying motives or causes. Makes inferences and finds evidence to support generalizations. Separates material or concepts into component parts so that its organizational structure may be understood. Distinguishes between facts and inferences.	Analyze	analyze assume categorize classify compare conclusion contrast discover dissect distinction distinguish	divide examine function inference inspect list motive relationships take part in test for theme	• Troubleshoots a problem using logical deduction • Lists components or parts of a whole • Names the function of something • Makes a distinction between two or more things • Classifies or categorizes a number of things • Draws a conclusion • Lists the parts of a whole

(continued)

Bloom's Cognitive Learning Levels *(continued)*

Cognitive Level	Verb	Key Words		Examples
Synthesis				
Compiles information in a different way by combining elements in a new pattern or proposing alternative solutions Builds a structure or pattern from diverse elements. Puts parts together to form a whole, with emphasis on creating a new meaning or structure.	Create	adapt arrange build categorize change choose combine compile compose construct create delete design develop devise discuss elaborate estimate explain formulate generate happen imagine improve	invent make up maximize minimize modify organize original originate plan predict propose rearrange reconstruct relate reorganize revise rewrite summarize solution solve suppose tell test write	• Integrates training from several sources to solve a problem • Formulates a theory • Invents a solution • Constructs a model • Compiles facts • Minimizes or maximizes an event or item • Designs a solution, model, or project • Adapts something to create another thing
Evaluation				
Presents and defends opinions by making judgments about information, validity of ideas, or quality of work based on a set of criteria.	Evaluate	agree appraise assess award choose compare conclude criteria	importance influence interpret judge justify mark measure opinion	• Selects the most effective solution • Explains a selection, conclusion, or recommendation • Prioritizes facts • Rates or ranks facts, characters (people), or events • Assesses the value or importance of something

Bloom's Cognitive Learning Levels *(continued)*

Cognitive Level	Verb	Key Words		Examples
Evaluation (continued) Makes judgments about the value of ideas or materials.		criticize decide deduct defend determine disprove dispute estimate evaluate explain	perceive prioritize prove rank rate recommend rule on select support value	• Justifies a selection, conclusion, or recommendation

Adapted from Benjamin S. Bloom, *Taxonomy of Educational Objectives: The Classification of Educational Goals, by a Committee of College and University Examiners* (New York: Longmans, Green, 1956).

The Standards

4

Standards-based education came into the national spotlight over a decade ago. Communities and school districts previously made their own curriculum choices. For example, in one school district civics was taught in eighth grade and in another district it was taught in ninth grade, resulting in uneven and low test scores, because children were not taught the same subjects in the same grades but were tested on the same subjects.

The idea behind the standards reform movement is straightforward: when states set clear standards defining what a child should know and be able to do in certain grades, teachers and learners are able to focus their efforts and highlight particular areas in which they need improvement. Ideally, the standards show teachers what they need to teach by allowing curricula and assessments that measure performance to be aligned with the standards.

As with all reform movements, there are people who disagree with the idea of creating common learning standards. They primarily point to tendencies to simply "teach the test" and complain that the standards limit content breadth and community input. The real gripe may lie in the fact that education has always been a local issue. It is easy to fear change when you fear community values may be lost by standard-izing state curriculum. Others believe that standards even the playing field. Before you form your own opinion, let's take a look at standards-based education.

Standards-based education lists content and skills that children need to learn at each grade level. Success depends on combining con-tent and performance standards with consistent curriculum and instruction as well as appropriate assessment and accountability. This is the point where teachers and learners start to feel anxious. Every-thing sounds very official, particularly the accountability part. What does this language mean and what happens if children don't meet learning standards requirements?

Relax—there are no learning standards police patrolling our neigh-borhood schools, libraries, and bookstores. There are simply baselines by which the state determines eligibility for a high school diploma.

Let's start by defining learning standards.

Types of Learning Standards

Learning standards are broad statements that describe what content a child should know and what skills a child should be able to do in different subject areas.

Content standards are a form of learning standards that describe the topics to be studied, not the skills to be performed.

Performance standards are a form of learning standards that describe the skills to be performed, not the content to be studied.

Public school teachers must ensure that their students are taught the required content and skills because they are accountable not only to the students but also to their state, their school district, and their commu-nity for every child's performance on test scores. Private schools are accountable to their constituency with respect to student performance but not to the public. In fact, school requirements as well as teacher licensure are not as strictly monitored for private schools. The academically strong private schools institute internal standards that meet or exceed state expectations for public schools, but there are private schools that feel other aspects of child development, such as religious development, take precedence over academics. If your child attends private school, you must research the school to make sure it meets your expectations both academically and socially.

The use of testing to monitor classroom instruction is central to the theory of standards-based reform. It assumes that educators and the public can agree on what should be taught, that a set of clear standards can be developed, which in turn drive curriculum and instruction, and that tests can measure how well students perform based on those standards. There are two main types of standardized testing that your child will encounter:

1. Tests to determine individual student eligibility for promotion and graduation, college admission, or special honors. This type of testing has a long history. Examples include high school exit exams and college entrance exams, such as the Scholastic Aptitude Test (SAT), and the Advanced Placement (AP) test.

2. Tests that measure and compare school, school district, statewide, and national performance for broad public accountability. Increasingly, policy makers at the federal, state, and local levels want to identify ways to measure student performance in order to see how well the public education system is doing its job. The goals of this accountability approach include providing information about the status of the educational system, motivating desired change, measuring program effectiveness, and creating systems for financially sanctioning schools and requiring educators to receive more training based on the performance of their students.

It makes sense for you to make sure the content and the skills that you work on with your child match the content and skills that the state has identified for that grade level. Children will do better on the standardized tests when more learning standards match assessment, or test, requirements. Legislation is in place that requires states to align their learning expectations with their testing expectations. The disconnect came when federal requirements for learning standards preceded testing requirements. Many states took the opportunity to test for content and skills that seemed more important than the ones enumerated in the learning standards. States and schools are working under federal guidelines to make all of the content match in a few years.

Learning Standards Resources

Each state has created a document that describes what children are supposed to know and what they are supposed to be able to do at each grade level and in each subject area. You may wonder who writes the standards and why you should believe that these people know what is best. A lot of public school teachers have wondered the same thing.

You can rest assured that writing the state learning standards is a collaborative effort. Most states rely on input from experts who know about the grade level and subject area. These experts could include teachers, researchers, people from the education industry, and school administrators. As an endnote or a footnote, each document lists the people hired by the state to help write the final version.

You can locate the standards that apply to your child through your state Department of Education's Internet site, by calling your state Department of Education, or through the Internet at www. knowledgeessentials.com. There are several things you should read for:

1. *Content standards*: What topics will your child be studying?
2. *Performance standards*: What skills must your child develop by the end of the year?

3. *Resources*: What resources are designed to help teachers meet the learning standards? Can you access them?

4. *Correlation reports*: Does the state provide a listing of how the required textbooks and other materials meet their own learning standards? Your school district should also be able to provide you with this information.

As you read your state's learning standards document, you may notice that you don't always agree with what is listed for your child to be learning. Is there anything you can do?

If your child attends a public school, there is little you can do to protest the prescribed curricula, but you can certainly enhance the curricula through learning activities at home. If your child attends a private school, you may have greater influence over classroom activities (as a paying customer), but you will probably not get the curricula changed to meet your concerns.

If you teach your child at home, then you have as much control as you would like over your child's curricula. You undoubtedly have specific beliefs that have led you to decide to homeschool, and you can remain true to those beliefs while still covering the required curricula. Even if you don't believe the required curricula are entirely appropriate, the assessments required by the states and higher education institutions will be normed to the learning standards of the state in which you live. The standards are just the basics that your child will need to succeed in mainstream society. There are many more opportunities for learning across a wide range of subjects that can be totally up to you.

Second Grade Reading 5

So, your child's reading! You're done, right? Not so fast! Things are just starting to get interesting. Second grade reading is a pretty important year for your child in developing the skill sets that allow him or her to see beyond the pronunciation of words to their meaning and implication. Comprehension is a set of learned skills that enables your child to understand new information. A certain amount of comprehension occurs naturally, but that only gets you so far—the rest is learned.

In second grade reading the focus changes from decoding (sounding out) words to learning the basic mechanics of reading. As your child grasps the mechanics of reading, comprehension skills come into greater focus.

Comprehension is also a bigger deal in second grade. It is one thing to know letters and sounds and figure out what they look like and how they sound when together, but

Beginning of Second Grade Reading Checklist

Students who are working at the standard level at the beginning of second grade:

____ Develop appropriate active strategies to construct meaning from print

____ Decode unfamiliar words

____ Understand how speech sounds are connected

____ Understand or are able to figure out (using contextual clues) the meaning of what they read

____ Develop and maintain motivation to read

____ Extend a story

____ Predict what will happen next

____ Discuss the character's motives

____ Question the author's meaning

____ Describe causes and effects of events in the text

____ Discuss books by tying their comments directly to the text it is a whole other thing to know what the word parts mean or to recognize them and know what they mean without thinking about it.

During second grade you will gradually see reading change from something your child learns to something he or she uses to learn. Your child will not only comprehend what he or she is reading, but be able to make conclusions from it as well.

The basic skill set for second grade reading is the mechanics of reading and comprehension. The following table will help put it into perspective.

Mechanics of Reading	Comprehension Skills
Recognizes word patterns, such as prefixes and suffixes	Reads with understanding and fluency
Utilizes a larger sight vocabulary	Recognizes important parts of a story, such as setting, characters, and plot
Figures out unknown words in context	Retells stories with accuracy
Identifies and spells many words	Draws conclusions based on readings

The Mechanics of Reading

There is a lot to cover in reading mechanics. We are going to focus on a few major concepts that are critical for second graders:

- Parts of words, such as prefixes and suffixes

- Vocabulary

- Context clues

By this point your child can decode (sound out words) and if he or she can't, then this inability is a red flag and needs attention. Once your child begins to sound out and read single words, he or she will start to try to read harder words. This is where the mechanics of reading come in.

Prefixes and Suffixes

Words are made up of prefixes, root words, and suffixes. A root word is a real word that can stand on its own and has a meaning. New words can be made from root words using prefixes and suffixes.

Root words are helpful because they can help your child decode what the entire word is and what it means in context. They can also help your child spell new words and begin to recognize patterns in words.

A prefix is a group of letters that is added to the beginning of a root word and changes the meaning of the word. Some common prefixes are un-, mis- and re-. As your child continues to read, he or she may start to notice that many words with mis- in front of them seem to mean something is wrong. Encourage your child to look for words that start with the same prefixes and discuss what they mean. Understanding the meanings of prefixes will help your little reader to figure out what the word means in a sentence.

Root words also can have suffixes, which are groups of letters added to the end of a word to change its meaning. Not only can a suffix change the meaning of a word, it can help your child understand how it is going to be used in a sentence. The most common suffixes are -ed and -ing. Your child will be able to pick out many words that end this way. The most confusing fact for your child will probably be that some suffixes change the spelling of the root word.

Vocabulary

If you had a choice between dragging your fingernails across a chalkboard twenty times in a row or looking up and learning twenty new vocabulary words, which would you choose? Had to think about it, didn't you? Do long lists of words that look like they're in another language and drills on the meanings, the spellings, and the parts of speech send chills up your spine?

Happily, most teachers today agree that the "drill and kill" or memorization method of learning vocabulary is not as effective as it once was thought to be. It is still pretty useful, but learning vocabulary is easier when your child knows the context that the new word is used in. Your child can expect to find vocabulary quizzes in his or her future, so it would be useful to get good at them now. Chances are that your child has vocabulary words for the things he or she is doing in science or social studies as well as words that match the literature in the reading program.

Context Clues

In order for your child's vocabulary to expand (and increase comprehension), he or she needs to read the words in context. How many times as a student in school did you hear your teacher say, "If you don't know a word, finish the sentence and come back to it"? When you were a child, that may have sounded pretty silly, but it does make sense. Sometimes you have to read the entire thing to get the gist and the meaning of the unknown word. That's using context clues.

Your child is probably doing this already and doesn't even know it. Children at this age are usually so eager to read on their own that they are unconsciously skimming the text and internalizing new words based on the whole sentence. The child who is more detailed and gets hung up on words he or she doesn't know will need to learn how to use context clues.

Selecting Reading Material

To help your child with reading, you need to use appropriate books. There are various reading levels within each grade level and codes on books to tell you what they are and what they mean. See appendix A and www.knowledgeessentials.com for a list of these books and to learn how to use them. Aside from fancy readability formulas and/or leveling procedures, when choosing reading material with your child, it is most important to consider his or her:

- Prior knowledge
- Past experience
- Interest in the subject
- Familiarity with the recommended age of the material

Other factors to consider include:

- Book length
- Book size
- Illustrations and graphics
- Type size and spacing
- Print layout

The following table lists some important skills related to the mechanics of reading, where children can run into problems, and what you can do to help them along.

Mechanics of Reading Skills	Having Problems?	Quick Tips
Can read a large amount of words automatically.	Cannot easily identify words by sight.	Make flash cards of words that your child struggles with, then practice, practice, practice!
Can identify and define word patterns, such as prefixes and suffixes.	Does not see the relevance between words with like beginnings and endings.	Examine words that have the same beginning or ending groups of letters. Look up the definitions to check for similarities.
Can read and understand parts of a story.	Reads with no comprehension of plot, setting, or conclusions.	Break stories down piece by piece and discuss who, what, where, when, and why.
Can make conclusions based on readings.	Conclusions are way off the mark.	Use graphic organizers, such as mapping out the important parts of the story.
Understands grade-appropriate vocabulary.	Has trouble retaining words with definitions.	Use vocabulary words in daily life as much as possible to reinforce meanings.

Mechanics of Reading Activities

1 New News

TIME: 20–30 minutes

MATERIALS
- newspaper
- highlighter
- nontoxic glue
- sheet of blank paper
- rounded-edge scissors
- dictionary

Take a page out of the newspaper and highlight words that your child can read and a few he can't. Highlight enough to make some sentences.

Learning happens when: you ask your child to say a highlighted word and then cut it out. Let your child paste the word onto the blank sheet of paper. When you and your child come to a word that is new, help your child to decode the word. Ask if he knows what the word means. If your child knows the meaning, it gets pasted onto the paper. If your child doesn't know what the word means, look it up in the dictionary with him and then add it to the sheet of words. Ask your child to write sentences using each word that has been pasted. Continue doing this until your child has his own newspaper to read.

Variations: help your child highlight words in the paper that he doesn't know, but would like to know. Ask your child to cut out each word and paste it onto a blank sheet of paper. He can then read the newspaper with your help. Work with your child on the new words and their meanings.

- Ask your child to show you how to use the dictionary and talk about how to use the pronunciation section next to each word.

- Look in the dictionary with your child. Show him the pronunciation section and ask him to read the pronunciation of a word. Explain to your child that the pronunciation key is a way that you can see what the word sounds like. Try another word and then ask your child to make a pronunciation key for a word that he knows well.

Ask your child to show you how to use the dictionary. Give him a list of three words to look up on his own. You can ask your child to tell you the definition or act it out.

Mastery occurs when: your child can correctly identify and pronounce each word and use it in a sentence. Your child should also be able to decode the new words and locate them in the dictionary.

You may want to help your child a little more if: your child cannot correctly identify and pronounce the words that you chose or cannot use them in a sentence. You can try to find easier words to start with, or make only one or two sentences to start with.

2 Root Word Families

Learning occurs when: you give your child a root word such as "add," "use," "clear," "act," "care." Ask your child to write down as many words as she can think of that have the root word in it. Let your child keep a record of how many root words she has found and add to it routinely.

Write a root word on a chalkboard or whiteboard and say it aloud. Ask your child to say as many words as she can think of with the root word in it. Write down those words.

Give your child a root word. Write down a few words; include one with the root word in it. See if your child can choose the one containing the root word.

Make some index cards with root words on them and make other cards with prefixes and suffixes on them. Place the

TIME: 15–20 minutes

MATERIALS
- list of words (your list of words can be from school or a list of words that your child had trouble with in other activities; if you don't have a list of words, you can find one that is appropriate for your child at www. knowledgeessentials.com)
- paper
- pencils

prefix or suffix cards beside the root word cards so that they don't make sense and ask your child to move the cards around until they do make sense.

Mastery occurs when: your child can pick out a majority of the words that have the root word in them.

You may want to help your child a little more if: she has difficulty thinking of words with the root word in it. You may want to help your child by writing down a few words with her.

3 Scrambled Words

TIME: 15–20 minutes

MATERIALS
paper
pencils

Learning happens when: you write a large word, such as "information," on the top of your child's paper. Ask him to make as many words as he can, using the letters in the big word. Mention that your child cannot add extra letters or double the letters. Also point out that there could be word families (cat, mat, hat), words with the same prefix or suffix, rhyming words, or words with the same base word (hope, hopes, hoped). Discuss the different patterns you and your child find. Check for correct spelling.

Variations: Use a variety of letters instead of a real word. Sometimes seeing a word stunts a child's ability to see other words. With a mix of letters, children are less likely to get stuck on the words.

- Talk it out with your child and give him hints for the bigger words he might not notice.
- Add interest by using a different color for each letter in the word. Not only will your child love the colors, it will help him to see the words that start with a certain letter.
- Definitely let your moving learner use magnetic letters or letter cards to do this activity.

Mastery occurs when: your child can identify words that use the letters from the original word and spell them correctly.

You may want to help your child a little more if: he is not able to make words out of the letters in the original word. If you are using a real word as the target word, scramble the letters for your child. Start the activity by picking out a few words that your child can build on with the other letters.

4 Vocabulary Songs

TIME: 30 minutes

MATERIALS
▪ favorite song of your child's
▪ dictionary

Learning happens when: you ask your child to sing you the song. Pick out words in the song that your child may not know. Ask if she knows what the word means. If not, sing the line with the word in it, putting it into context. Use the dictionary with your child to find the word and what it means. Sing the song with your child using the new information and then go back and check with her to see if she remembers the word and its meaning.

Variations: Make two copies of the words to a song that your child knows and sings routinely. Take your copy and highlight words that your child may not know. Give your child the other copy and sing the song. Then ask your child what the highlighted words mean. If your child doesn't know, read the whole line the word is in, or use the dictionary to find the definition. Sing the song again and check for comprehension by asking your child once more what the word means in the song.

🕉 Try this activity with a favorite poem or rhyming storybook. Dr. Seuss might be a little difficult for this because of the use of made-up words. Stick to something that uses real words.

👁 Ask your child to read the words to a song or to read a story to you. When your child finds words that are new or that your child doesn't know the definitions of, ask her to write them down on a sheet of paper. Look up the definitions together and then reread the song or story.

✌ Dance, I said, dance! Add movement (with rhythm) to the song.

Mastery occurs when: your child can define the words you chose and can explain how they fit in the song.

You may want to help your child a little more if: your child can't explain what the words mean in relation to the song. You may want to take the song, line by line, and discuss what the song is about so that your child has a better understanding. Many times, songs are rote memory, and the meanings are not involved in the memory. This activity will help children to understand what they are singing about.

5 Swat It!

TIME: 15–20 minutes

Write the vocabulary words on the index cards. Tape them to a wall in a few rows.

Learning happens when: you give your child the flyswatter and explain that you are going to read the definition of a word, and when you say "Swat it!" your child will take the flyswatter and smack the word that goes with the definition.

Variations: If you'd rather not have your child whacking the wall, you can transfer this activity to a table. Tape the words down and let your child slap his hand down over the correct word.

🦻 Instead of swatting the word, you can have your child shout it out to you.

👁 Rather than swatting the word, ask your child to write it on a whiteboard or a sheet of paper and show it to you.

✋ This activity is perfect for kinesthetic learners—use it as written with confidence!

Mastery occurs when: your child successfully associates the definitions you are saying to the words on the wall.

You may want to help your child a little more if: he is having trouble finding the word that goes with the definition. Start with fewer words and slowly introduce one new card after every two or three your child gets correct, until he can work up to the full set of words.

MATERIALS
▪ list of vocabulary words with definitions (your list of words can be from school or a list of words that your child had trouble with in other activities; if you don't have a list of words, you can find one that is appropriate for your child at www.knowledgeessentials.com)
▪ index cards
▪ marker
▪ flyswatter
▪ dictionary
▪ tape

6 | Vocabulary Charades

Write one vocabulary word on each slip of paper and put the pieces of paper into a hat or a box.

Learning happens when: you model for your child how to play the game. Pick a slip out of the box and act it out. Remember, there's no talking. Give yourself thirty seconds to try to act out the word for your child. If your child figures it out, good for you! If not, say the word and ask her for the definition. Switch roles and play again.

Variations: Use the definitions on the slips instead of the words and see if your child can act them out.

🦻 If charades is not for you or your auditory learner, try clue words. Instead of acting the word out, try choosing

TIME: 30 minutes

MATERIALS
▪ list of vocabulary words with definitions (your list of words can be from school or a list of words that your child had trouble with in other activities; if you don't have a list of words, you can find one that is appropriate for your child at www.knowledgeessentials.com)
▪ hat or box
▪ marker
▪ slips of paper
▪ stopwatch

a word and giving your child clue words to see if she can identify it.

👁 Pictionary, anyone? If you've got a visual learner, try drawing pictures to figure out the word.

✋ What is better for a moving learner than charades? Use this activity without any changes.

Mastery occurs when: your child can guess the word or the definition when you act it out.

You may want to help your child a little more if: she is having trouble identifying the acted-out word. Give your child a hint, like the first letter of the word.

7 Go Fish

TIME: 15–30 minutes

MATERIALS
▪ list of vocabulary words (your list of words can be from school or a list of words that your child had trouble with in other activities; if you don't have a list of words, you can find one that is appropriate for your child at www. knowledgeessentials.com)
▪ index cards
▪ markers

Create your own deck of Go Fish cards using the vocabulary words. Write each word on two index cards.

Learning happens when: you mix up the cards and divide them equally between you and your child. Each set of word cards is a pair that you can take out of your deck. Begin by asking your child if he has a certain word card by giving him the definition. If the answer is yes, he will give the card to you. If the answer is no, he says "Go fish." Then, your child will do the same to you. When you are finished and all the cards have been paired, ask your child to go through them and spell each word.

👂 The rules of the game reinforce learning through talking and hearing—your child will do well with this activity as it is.

👁 Use colored index cards for different types of words. Use blue for verbs, red for nouns, yellow for adjectives, and so forth.

Not only can you play for vocabulary and spelling enrichment, you can also use this activity to strengthen grammar skills.

The act of playing cards couples learning through movement. This activity is good for your kinesthetic learner as it is.

Mastery occurs when: your child can successfully identify each definition and spell each word.

You may want to help your child a little more if: he is having trouble matching the words or spelling them. Start with fewer words or review the words before you start the game.

8 Definition Cereal Words

Write the definition of each word on a separate card.

Learning happens when: you sit down with your child and look over the list of words. Show your child a card, reading the definition if needed. Ask your child to use the alphabet cereal to spell out the word that goes with that definition.

Variations: Use alphabet pasta. Write the words on the cards and have your child write out the definitions in cereal or pasta.

Ask your child to spell the word aloud before she spells out the word with the cereal.

When your child has finished spelling the word with the cereal, ask her to write out the word on a sheet of paper.

Manipulating the alphabet cereal will give your child the opportunity to learn through movement. Add more actions

TIME: 15–20 minutes

MATERIALS
- list of vocabulary words (your list of words can be from school or a list of words that your child had trouble with in other activities; if you don't have a list of words, you can find one that is appropriate for your child at www.knowledgeessentials.com)
- alphabet cereal
- marker
- index cards

by asking your child to glue the cereal onto paper to spell the words.

Mastery occurs when: your child can successfully match the definition with the word and spell the words correctly.

You may want to help your child a little more if: she is having difficulty identifying or spelling the word. Give your child the starting letter.

9 Basketball

TIME: 15–20 minutes

MATERIALS
- a clean bucket or garbage can
- masking tape
- paper
- list of vocabulary words (your list of words can be from school or a list of words that your child had trouble with in other activities; if you don't have a list of words, you can find one that is appropriate for your child at www. knowledgeessentials.com)

Set up the bucket or garbage can about twenty feet away from your child. Tape three lines to the floor between your child and the bucket or can. Create a tape ball by crumpling up some paper until it's about the size of a baseball and winding tape around it to secure it.

Learning happens when: you give your child the ball and a definition. If your child gets the word right, he can either choose to move up a line or take a shot. If your child gets the word wrong, he should step back a line.

Variations: Give your child the word and ask her for the definition.

- After your child has identified the word, ask him to spell it.
- It may help your visual learner to actually *see* the definition you're saying. Write the definitions out on large sheets of paper and show them to your child as you say the definition.
- This lesson stands as is as a great activity for kinesthetic learners.

Mastery occurs when: your child can identify each word in the list correctly.

You may want to help your child a little more if: he cannot identify the word from the definition. Start by reading the list aloud before you begin, or leave a list visible so that your child can choose from one of the words.

10 Pick-Up Sticks

Make a set of pick-up sticks by writing words from the list on the back and front of the craft sticks.

Learning happens when: you hold the sticks up together and let them drop onto the table or floor. Your child will then say the word on the stick she wants to pick up and try to remove the stick without moving another stick. If she removes a stick successfully, she keeps it and continues. If your child identifies the word incorrectly or moves another stick, she loses her turn and you go. Continue until all the sticks have been picked up.

Variations: Write the definition on one stick and the word on another. Ask your child to match the sticks and pick up both.

TIME: 20–30 minutes

MATERIALS
- list of vocabulary words (your list of words can be from school or a list of words that your child had trouble with in other activities; if you don't have a list of words, you can find one that is appropriate for your child at www. knowledgeessentials.com)
- craft sticks
- marker

- Saying the word as your child picks the appropriate stick is the component that fits your aural learner, but you can add to the learning by asking your child to tell the definition of the words she picks up.

- If the printed word isn't quite enough to teach your visual learner new words, make a list of the words to keep on the floor by the game and ask your child to put a checkmark by the words she picks up.

- Picking up the sticks while saying the word is great for kinesthetic learners, but you can reinforce the meanings of the new words by asking your child to look up the definition in the dictionary and then act it out.

Mastery occurs when: your child can successfully say the words on the sticks that she picks up.

You may want to help your child a little more if: your child has difficulty matching the words to the definitions. Start off with a smaller amount of words and gradually build the number of sticks.

Comprehension

Your child can read words and usually knows what those words mean—but does he or she know what they mean when they are beside each other in a sentence?

How do you know if things are making sense to your child and he or she is internalizing what he or she is reading? Comprehension is broken down into subsections, and second graders are working on language, concentration, and memory.

Language

There is no reason not to acknowledge the elephant in the room—the English language is one of the hardest to learn. Just when your child has gotten used to sounding out the words, putting them together, and figuring out what they mean, he or she has to start reading more difficult sentence structures and punctuation, all with rules and, of course, exceptions. It can be a little confusing, but your child can and will do it. After all, you did!

Concentration (Focus)

Have you ever started to read a book and then after page three realized that it was so boring or confusing that you didn't remember anything you read so far? That memory can help you to understand what your child may be feeling as the materials he or she is reading become more involved, more detailed, and more varied in topic. It takes a lot of energy and focus to start reading something, let alone finishing it.

Concentrating on what they're reading is what helps children retain and retell information. It also helps them quickly pick up on key information, such as titles, italicized words, bold print, and other differences that mark importance. This ability to focus will also help them to sort out the important information versus the filler in what they are reading. Concentration helps them to become more efficient readers because they "get it" the first time.

Memory

It's something that kids usually have too much of while we sorely lack it. Memories are the key to your child relating new information to old information. As children read, they are learning to retain what's important and filter out the insignificant. They also need to hold onto that information so that later on they can relate it to something new.

Comprehending what you are reading is the most important part of that activity—but it can't be achieved without phonics, language, and the other skills your child is learning on a daily basis. Comprehension will become even more important as the subject areas become more advanced and varied. Every subject that your child has from now until graduation will require a detailed understanding based on reading. If your child doesn't have a solid grasp on reading skills during second grade, third grade will be difficult, and the rest of the grades will be a combination of frustration, anxiety, and mediocre achievement. But don't worry. If you and your child work diligently on reading skills in partnership with the teacher this year, your child will likely be well prepared for the challenges ahead.

The table on page 54 shows some of the skills needed to successfully comprehend readings, where children can run into problems, and what you can do to help them along.

Comprehension Skills	Having Problems?	Quick Tips
Can read and retain information at the same time.	Does not remember the beginning of a story by the time he or she reaches the end.	Ask your child to read to you. Ask questions during the reading to see what details and information he or she can remember.
Can read and store information and recall it at a later time.	Does not retain information enough to recall later.	Outlines—the best skill you can ever have. Help your child make simple outlines listing information that seems important to the story.
Can make reasonable inferences and conclusions about his or her reading.	Makes no logical conclusions about readings; cannot infer from reading.	Ask your child to read stories he or she is familiar with. Find a topic of interest outside of the assigned reading.

Comprehension Activities

1 Comic Strip Mix-Up

TIME: 10–15 minutes

MATERIALS
- your child's favorite comic strip or comic book
- rounded-edge scissors

Take your child's favorite comic strip (or a section of the comic book) and cut each individual cell apart.

Learning occurs when: you mix up the cells and ask your child to put them back in order and then read the comic to you.

- You can do this activity (without the scissors) with a favorite short story your child likes. Read the story to your child, but read the pages out of order. Ask your child to tell you the correct order of events.

- Take out the last cell of the comic strip. After your child puts the strip together, ask if there is anything missing. When your child says that the ending is not there, have him write a new ending and draw a picture that goes with it.

Ask your child to make his own comic strip and to cut it apart. Your child should mix up the cells or boxes, and then you can try to put them in order. When you can't (and, believe me, it is highly likely that you won't be able to) ask your child to put them in the proper order and tell you about them.

Mastery occurs when: your child can reconstruct the sequence of the story.

You may want to help your child a little more if: he cannot put the comic back in order. Check to see if your child can read each cell, and if so, let him look at the pictures for help. If your child cannot understand each cell individually, show him the comic strip *before* you begin.

2 | And the Moral of the Story Is . . .

Learning occurs when: you read a fable to your child. Read the story, but stop before the moral and the ending of the story. Ask your child to tell you what the lesson of the fable is based on the story so far. Then read the rest of the story. Let your child tell you how her ending was different or the same.

TIME: 20–30 minutes

MATERIALS
- fable

- Talk with your child about the moral of the fable. Ask questions such as: Why do you think that people write stories with a moral? Can you think of any other stories or fables that have a moral?

- Ask your child to write her own moral and ending to the story. Compare it to the actual ending and discuss.

- Let your child act out the story's moral and ending.

Mastery occurs when: your child can follow the story and make predictions about the moral and the ending.

You may want to help your child a little more if: her prediction is far off the mark or your child is having trouble following the story. Go back to the beginning of the story and discuss the main points. Ask your child to try to make a conclusion about the ending and what the lesson in the story is about.

3 | Taking Turns Tale

TIME: 30 minutes

MATERIALS
- paper
- pencils

Learning happens when: you and your child come up with a fun title for a story. Brainstorm with him about what kinds of characters would be in the story and what would happen. Then ask your child to write the first sentence in the story. You write the second, and so on, taking turns until the story is complete.

Variations: Ask your child to write the first sentence. When you write your sentence, leave one word blank. Ask your child to read the sentence and find a word to fill in the blank. Continue this way until you have finished the story.

- Start this activity by saying each sentence aloud, preferably into a tape recorder, which will help your auditory learner to formulate his ideas. Then, help him to transfer those ideas to paper.

- Once your story is complete, ask your child to create the cover for your story, including the title, the authors, and an illustration.

- Act out a sentence for your child to interpret and write down. The sentence may not reflect exactly what you're trying to act out, but that's okay because it allows your child to be creative. Then switch roles.

Mastery occurs when: your child can complete the next sentence in the story while staying within the theme of the story and the preceding sentence.

You may want to help your child a little more if: the sentences are not consistent with the story line. Read the story so far and discuss what your child might want to write next. This will help your child stay within the story line.

4 | Story Map

Learning happens when: you ask your child to tell you about a story you have read recently. Ask your child to draw a medium-sized circle in the middle of the paper. Have her write the name of the storybook in the circle. Ask your child to draw four lines from the circle, leaving room to write around each line. Ask for the names of the important people in the story. Help your child label one of the lines "Characters" and spell the names of the characters beneath it. Sound out the words and write labels in the same way for "Setting," "Problem," and "Ending."

TIME: 20–30 minutes

MATERIALS
- recently read storybook
- paper
- pencils

Variations: Try this activity with a new book.

- Talk with your child extensively before creating the chart. An auditory learner needs to vocalize her thoughts before transferring them to paper.

- Before starting the chart, reread the story with your child to make sure that the information is fresh in her mind.

- Try making paper-sack puppets that represent characters in the story. Ask your child to retell the story to you using the puppets that she has made.

Mastery occurs when: your child can correctly identify key elements in the story and retell them.

You may want to help your child if: recalling the information is difficult. Reread the story and then try again. If necessary, let your child use the book as a reference.

5 Sentence Pictures

TIME: 10–15 minutes

MATERIALS

crayons

big paper

Learning happens when: you read your child the following sentence: The box fell. Brainstorm with your child how many sentences you can make by adding in adjectives: The big box fell. The orange box fell. Write the sentences on big paper with crayons. Let him read the sentences aloud.

Variations: Try this activity with verbs and adverbs: The box fell fast. The box fell hard.

👂 When your child has finished writing out his sentences, ask him to read them aloud and point to the descriptive adjectives he added.

👁 Ask your child to draw pictures of the noun in the sentence that shows the way the adjective made it look. Match the pictures to the sentences.

✋ Change the sentence to be an active sentence that your child can act out: The box fell from my hands. I dropped the box. Ask him to act out as many variations as he can think of.

Mastery occurs when: your child can attach describing words to a sentence to create new sentences.

You may want to help your child a little more if: your child has difficulty adding descriptive words to the sentence. Ask questions such as, What kind of box could it be? Where is the box? Where did it fall?

6 Pausing Punctuation

Write a few sentences with different types of punctuation. Use periods, commas, exclamation points, semicolons, and question marks.

TIME: 15–20 minutes

MATERIALS
- paper
- pencils

Learning happens when: you read the sentences to your child, overemphasizing the punctuation. Ask your child what the punctuation tells you about how to read the sentences. Point out the different types of punctuation. Ask your child to read the sentences in the same way—overemphasizing the punctuation—while putting her finger on the punctuation marks as they come up.

Variations: Ask your child to write and read to you a funny passage using different punctuation marks.

- Try this same activity with a favorite song. Give your child the words to the song to follow along with and sing with exaggerated expressions while your child points to the punctuation in the song.

- Ask your child to write and read to you a passage using the new punctuation that shows excitement.

- Write a list of actions that correspond with the punctuation. As your child reads the list, ask her to do the action that matches the punctuation.

Mastery occurs when: your child can correctly read and use punctuation.

You may want to help your child a little more if: she is having problems identifying or articulating punctuation. Start with just one type of punctuation in a passage until your child has a better grasp and then move on to a new one.

7 | KWL Reading

TIME: 20–30 minutes

MATERIALS

■ paper
■ pencils
■ a book on a topic of interest to your child (it's best if the book is new to your child)

Learning begins when: you ask your child to fold the paper into three columns and label them: "Know," "Want to Know," and "Learned." Show your child the book and ask him what he knows about it, based on the cover and prior knowledge. For example, if the book is about cats, what does your child know about cats? Ask your child to list everything he knows about the topic under the "Know" column. Under the "Want to Know" column, ask your child to write down things that he would like to know about the topic of the book. Ask your child to read the book. After reading the book, ask your child to fill out the "Learned" column with everything learned from the book. See the sample chart on page 61. You can find a blank know/want/learn (KWL) chart at www.knowledgeessentials.com.

Variations: Ask your child to make an information web instead of a KWL chart. Put the title of the book in the middle and all new information stemming off the circle. See the sample web on page 61. You can find a blank information web at www.knowledgeessentials.com.

🦻 If your child is an auditory learner, you should discuss the book with him before having him fill out the KWL chart. Talking it out helps an auditory learner organize everything before putting it down on paper.

Sample KWL Chart for *Eloise*

Know	Want to Know	Learned
Eloise lives at the Plaza	What is the Plaza?	hotel
	Where is the Plaza?	NYC
Eloise has a pet turtle	How do you take care of a turtle?	food, water
	What food does a turtle eat?	grasses, flowers, worms, bugs, berries

Sample Information Web for *Eloise*

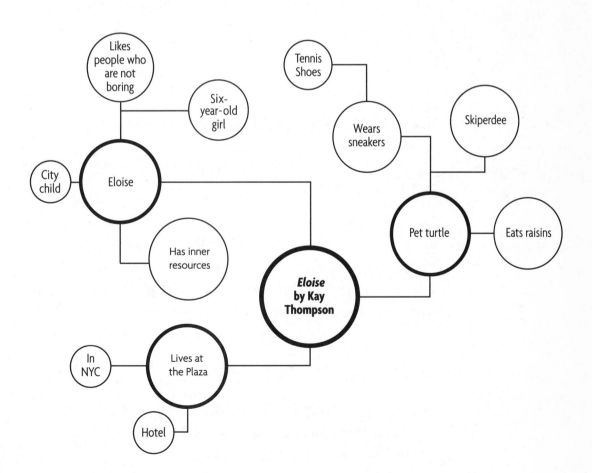

👁 After your child writes out the information, it may be helpful for your visual learner to add some illustrations to the chart.

✋ Add movement to the chart. For example, *K* can mean clap for what you know; *W* can mean wave for what you want to learn; and *L* can mean listen to what was learned.

Mastery occurs when: your child can correctly write down the information he has learned from the book.

You may want to help your child a little more if: he is not able to retain the information. Ask your child to write down the new facts as he reads, rather than at the end, and then explain them to you using examples from the reading.

8 | What's Wrong with These Sentences?

TIME: 20–30 minutes

MATERIALS
▪ markers
▪ paper
▪ passage from your child's favorite story

Rewrite a few sentences of the story, removing all the capitalization and punctuation.

Learning happens when: you show your child the sentences and ask her what is wrong with them. When your child notices that there is no punctuation or capitalization, ask her to fix what is wrong. After your child has made the edits, go through the sentences together, make any other edits she may have missed, and discuss.

Variations: Ask your child to write a passage for you to correct.

👂 After your child has edited the sentences, ask her to read them aloud. The punctuation will dictate how the sentences will sound.

- 👁 Ask your child to find another passage and take out the punctuation and capitalization for *you* to edit. When you're finished, give the paper back to your child to correct.

- ✍ Act it out! Once the sentences are edited, don't just *read* them, act them out so that your active child can associate the punctuation with the movement.

Mastery occurs when: your child can make the necessary grammatical corrections to the passage.

You may want to help your child a little more if: she is having trouble identifying the grammar mistakes. Start with missing capitalization, then do the punctuation later. Try using just one sentence at a time.

Environmental Learning

Kids say the darnedest things—and most of the time they learn them through their environment, be it television, signs along the road, even little things like a cereal box. Anything written anywhere can be used as a learning experience. Take your child to the mall. What do the parking lot signs read? What is the name of that store? What is this meal on the menu? Your child can read all sorts of things if you think to ask.

Reading should be part of your child's daily routine, and you should be involved. Whether it's reading to or with your child, listening to your child, or reading for yourself, the more your child is immersed in an environment that promotes reading, the more apt he or she is to be a better reader.

Children's abilities and expectations in reading are going to be growing just as fast as they. Being able to identify words quickly and correctly, looking for patterns, and then understanding the content becomes more important as they delve into a wider variety of subjects.

End of Second Grade Reading Checklist

Students who are working at the standard level at the end of second grade:

_____ Read with understanding and fluency

_____ Figure out unknown words in context

_____ Recognize word patterns (prefixes and suffixes)

_____ Communicate in writing

_____ Retell stories with accuracy

_____ Correct themselves while reading

_____ Identify and spell many words

_____ Recognize parts of a story

_____ Read for more than pleasure

_____ Use a larger sight vocabulary

Second Grade Writing   6

Second grade writing is an improvement on that of first grade because your child can write letters and make words. As you know, however, writing is not only a physical act but also a combination of previous information being used in new ways. This chapter will give you some ideas for helping your child expand his or her writing abilities and gain some new ones.

How many bits and sheets of paper do you have at home on which your child "wrote" something for you? Some of the early writing is crayon scribbles that say "I love you," although you and your child are probably the only ones who can read it. After

Beginning of Second Grade Writing Checklist

Students who are working at the standard level at the beginning of second grade:

_____ Communicate in writing

_____ Reread their writing to monitor meaning

_____ Begin to use feedback to change their writing—either by adding more text or by making minor revisions

_____ Insert text in the middle of their writing rather than just at the end

_____ Make deliberate choices about the language they use

_____ Use punctuation and capitalization more often than not

a time, some of your child's writings had actual letters in them, even small words like "Mom" or "Dad." By the end of first grade, your child was probably writing full sentences.

In second grade, children will continue to further their writing skills by including more detailed aspects of grammar and style. They will be asked to read and write a variety of writing structures, such as letters, plays, and poems. They will also be introduced to a new writing style: cursive. Instead of just getting their thoughts down on paper, children will begin writing with a purpose.

Writing Style and Grammar

A large majority of writing in second grade is about writing style, which consists of word choices and formats. In second grade, children will begin to read and write a variety of things, and it is generally the first time children will be asked to write book reports, demonstrating reading comprehension with writing skills. Children will read a book and then write about it in a format given by the teacher. They will write about the major events, characters, settings, and their opinions, and make conclusions about the story. They also may be introduced to interviews, plays, poems, biographies, and other types of writing.

The variety of words and their uses in the English language is mind-boggling, especially in second grade, when children learn how one word can have many meanings, spellings, and tenses and then apply that knowledge to their writing. They also will start to pick out nouns, adjectives, verbs, and adverbs and use them in their writing.

The table on page 69 describes some of the important skills related to writing style and grammar, where children can run into problems, and what you can do to help them along.

Because grammar has so many rules, it can often be frustrating to learn. So let's just hunker down and get through it so that your child will make sense to the outside world. Helping him or her grapple with grammar can get confusing, so let's take a look at some grammar concepts that you should be prepared to help your child with, now and for the next ten years.

Basic Grammar Concepts

Helping your child grapple with grammar can get confusing, so let's take a look at two grammar concepts that you should be prepared to help your child with, now and for the next ten years: the basic parts of speech, and sentence fundamentals.

The Basic Parts of Speech

adjective   A word that modifies a noun; it describes a quality of a person, place, or thing.

adverb   A word that describes a verb, adjective, or another adverb; it often ends in *ly*.

conjunction   "Junction what's your function? Hookin' up words and phrases and clauses." As the classic *Schoolhouse Rock* song tells us, conjunctions are words such as "and," "or," and "but" that connect words, ideas, phrases, clauses, and sentences into one big sentence or idea.

interjection   An exclamation or utterance such as "wow," "oh," or "huh."

noun   Names a person, place, thing, feeling, idea, or act.

plural noun   Refers to two or more people, places, or things.

proper noun   Names a particular person (someone's name), place, or thing and begins with a capital letter.

preposition   Shows the relationship between one noun and a different noun, verb, or adverb, such as "in" or "through."

pronoun   Replaces a noun, such as "he," "they," or "it."

singular noun   Refers to one person, place, or thing.

verb   Describes action.

verb tense   Tells you when the action happened. The main forms are present (I sing), past (I sang), future (I will sing), present participle (I am singing), and past participle (I have sung).

Sentence Fundamentals

What makes a sentence? For a group of words to be a sentence it needs three things:

1. The words make sense and express a complete thought.

(continued)

2. It begins with a capital letter and ends with a period, exclamation point, or question mark.

3. It contains a predicate and a subject. The predicate, or verb, tells what the subject, or noun, is doing.

Sentences can be any length, as long as they follow these rules.

The parts of a sentence include:

direct object   A noun or pronoun that is having an action done to it.

indirect object   A noun or pronoun that tells you for what or whom the action of the verb (predicate) is being done.

predicate   The verb that describes what the noun (subject) of the sentence is doing or being.

subject   A noun or pronoun that is performing the verb; the "doer" of a sentence.

The following are examples of subject and predicate:

1. Alice wins the race.

   Alice is the subject; *wins* is the predicate; *race* is the direct object.

2. Doug gave David two tickets.

   Doug is the subject; *gave* is the predicate; *David* is the indirect object; *tickets* is the direct object.

A **compound sentence** is two sentences joined together using a conjunction. The most common conjunctions are "and," "although," "as," "because," "but," "if," "or," "though," "where," and "whether." Conjunctions that indicate time are: *before, after, until, since, when, whenever,* and *while.*

The following sentences show how conjunctions are used:

Amy sold the blue coat *and* it was dirty.

Amy sold the blue coat *because* it was dirty.

Amy sold the blue coat *before* it was dirty.

Notice how the conjunctions change the meaning of the sentence, so choosing the right one is important!

Writing Style and Grammar Skills	Having Problems?	Quick Tips
Can identify parts of speech.	Has difficulty differentiating parts of speech.	Use basic sentences and identify each part of speech with different colors of ink.
Understands what each part of speech does.	Cannot define what each part of speech does.	Pick nouns and verbs out of every sentence that you can.
Reads and comprehends other types of literature (poems, interviews, biographies, articles).	Has difficulty reading literature other than stories.	Model reading for your child. Open a magazine or a book and look at the formats with your child, explaining what it means.
Incorporates new words and formats in writing.	Uses only basic writing elements (small words, short sentences).	Read your child's writing. Ask if there is another word he or she can think of to replace a basic word.

Writing Style and Grammar Activities

1 Magic Story

Place the pictures inside the box.

Learning happens when: you explain to your child that writing a story is like magic. It lets your child create and control the story, the characters, and where it all happens. Discuss the plot, setting, and characters in a story. What is a setting? What do characters do in a story? What is a plot? Ask your child to take a sheet of paper and fold it into three columns, and label each column with "Character," "Setting," and "Plot." Pull one of the pictures of people out of the box. Ask your child if it is part of the setting or the plot, or a character. Let your child write the person's name or job (for example, a policeman) in the correct column. Continue to pick out pictures and ask your child to list them under the proper

TIME: 20–30 minutes

MATERIALS
- paper
- pencils
- box
- three pictures of people
- three pictures of fun or exotic places
- three pictures of real or imaginary problems or situations

label. Talk with your child about what type of characters, settings, and plot he would use in a story. Ask him to write out the beginning of a story with the elements you discussed.

Variations: Read a story that is of interest to your child. Ask your child to create the three columns and on his own write down the characters, settings, and plot of that story.

- 👂 After your child writes the beginning of a story, ask him to read it to you.

- 👁 Read a story with your child and ask him to draw two characters, two settings, and two situations and write a sentence about each.

- ✋ Ask your child to finish his story. If it's too much for your child to write, have your child tell you how it ends.

Mastery occurs when: your child can correctly identify and use the basic elements of a story.

You may want to help your child a little more if: he has difficulty picking out the characters, setting, and plot. Practice looking for *just* the characters in books, then *just* the setting, and finally the plot. If your child is having trouble writing down his ideas, ask him to explain them in detail verbally and help him to write them down.

2 Mr. Nicholas Noun and Ms. Violet Verb

Draw the outline of a man on one sheet of paper and the outline of a woman on another (think bathroom signs). Make sure they are big enough that your child will be able to write on and around the drawing.

Learning happens when: you help your child write "Mr. Nicholas Noun" on the male drawing and "Ms. Violet Verb" on the female drawing. On the noun paper your child should write the nouns of the parts of the body (nose, elbow, finger). On the verb paper your child should write the verbs that correspond with different parts of the body (for example, "eat" would go near the mouth). Let your child read each picture to you after it is labeled. Hang the pages somewhere that your child can see to refer to when writing.

TIME: 20 minutes

MATERIALS
- paper
- pencils
- rounded-edge scissors

- Try this activity verbally. Give your child the name of a body part and ask her to think of an action that corresponds with it. Then, ask your child to figure out the body part that corresponds to the verb you say.

- Point to a part on your body and ask your child to write down a few verbs that correspond to the noun you're pointing to. Switch to actions and ask your child to write down the verb that applies. For example, point your foot and ask your child to write down a few verbs that happen with a foot. Foot verbs include walk, run, point, flex, stand, jump, spin, etc.

- Use a life-size model. Get two large sheets of paper and ask your child to lie down so that you can trace her on each piece. Then, fill in the verbs and nouns.

Mastery occurs when: your child can correctly list verbs and nouns.

You may want to help your child a little more if: she can only think of a few of each. For help with nouns, point to different parts of your body. For verbs, act things out.

3 | Mini Bios

TIME: 30–40 minutes

MATERIALS
- books with an "about the author" section
- picture of your child
- picture of yourself
- paper
- pencils

Learning happens when: you ask your child to look through the various books for the "about the author" section. After your child has found a few examples, talk about why some books have them. Do they all have pictures? What kinds of information do they include? Explain to your child that this is a type of biography. A biography is information someone writes about another person. You should also mention that there are also autobiographies, which are written by the person they are about. Brainstorm with your child and make a list of important information that should be included in his biography as well as your own. This is a great way for your child to learn more about you, too! Write each other's biographies and then attach the picture. You can ask your child to read his biography to you or act it out.

Variations: Ask your child to write his autobiography. You can share stories about your child when he was younger. This is something that your child can add to throughout his childhood.

- If your child is an auditory learner, try making an audiotape biography. Have your child use the list of information as an outline for what he will say.

- Make a picture biography. Gather as many photos as possible of you as a child and up through adulthood and a number of your child's photos (make sure they're ones you won't mind gluing to paper). Help your child put the photos in chronological order and then paste them onto individual sheets of paper. If your child doesn't already know, share with him what was going on when each picture was taken. Then, ask your child to write one or two sentences beneath the pictures.

When your child is finished, have him make a cover for the book.

✋ Visit family members to expand on this activity. It's amazing how much *you'll* discover about your family!

Mastery occurs when: your child can identify and use biographical information to write a biography.

You may want to help your child a little more if: he switches between third person (he, she, it) and first person (I, me, my). Explain that biographies are written in third person because you are writing about someone else. An autobiography is written in first person because you are writing about yourself.

4 | Goofy Greg

Learning happens when: you write the following on the board:

Goofy Greg likes chairs, but not sitting.

He likes food, but not eating.

He likes beds, but not sleeping.

He likes books, but not reading.

He likes songs, but not singing.

He likes water, but not swimming.

TIME: 20 minutes

MATERIALS
▪ chalkboard or white-board
▪ chalk or whiteboard markers

Ask your child if there is a pattern. Ask what kind of pattern she sees. What kinds of words are in the first part of the sentences? What kinds of words are in the second part of the sentences? Goofy Greg likes nouns, but not verbs!

Variations: Ask your child to write some of her own silly sentences that follow the noun/verb pattern.

👂 Try this activity aurally. Say each line aloud instead of writing it on the board.

👁 If your child learns better visually, say each line aloud while your child writes it down on the board.

✋ Take this activity outside on the sidewalk. If your child likes to move around, this will give her the opportunity while writing down the sentences with chalk.

Mastery occurs when: your child can differentiate between nouns and verbs in the sentence.

You may want to help your child a little more if: she doesn't see the pattern in the sentences. Start off with each sentence individually and dissect it with your child by picking out the nouns and verbs. Move on to the next sentence and do the same. After a few sentences, ask your child if she is starting to notice a pattern.

5 Jumpin' Parts of Speech!

TIME: 20 minutes

MATERIALS
▪ list of short sentences

Learning happens when: you choose a part of speech to work on with your child. For this example, let's use nouns. Ask your child to stand up. Explain that you are going to read a sentence. Every time your child hears a noun in the sentence he will jump up in the air. Read a list of short sentences and watch for your child to jump at the correct time.

Variations: Ask your child to listen for nouns *and* verbs, using different movements for each. Ask your child to do jumping jacks for the verbs and pat his or her head for nouns. Add in adjectives and adverbs, too.

☞ Is your child a better listening learner? Then this activity will appeal to him as is—all your child needs to do is listen!

👁 Make flash cards of the sentences. Show one to your child and ask him to read it and then jump as many times as there are nouns in the sentence.

✋ This activity is totally geared toward your kinesthetic learner. Keep on doing it just the way it was written.

Mastery occurs when: your child can pick out the particular part of speech you chose.

You may want to help your child a little more if: he is missing the words. It may help your child to actually see the words. Write them out on a chalkboard or whiteboard.

6 | Friendly Poetry

TIME: 30 minutes

MATERIALS
- pencils
- paper
- crayons or markers

Learning happens when: you talk to your child about friendship. What is friendship? What things does your child look for in a friend? How should a friend act? Write down all the ideas you both come up with. Then, ask your child to write a poem about friends using the list of ideas. Remind your child that poems don't have to rhyme.

Variations: Ask your child to write an acrostic poem about friends. An acrostic poem uses the letters in a word to start each line of the poem. Write the word "friends" down the left hand side of the page and ask your child to write something about friends that starts with each letter.

☞ Ask your child to read her poem to you and explain it.

👁 Ask your child to rewrite the poem neatly on a sheet of paper. Leave room at the top so that your child can illustrate the poem.

✋ Ask your child to gather some toys and other things that remind her of one specific friend or many friends. Your child should then write a poem about a friend or friends that mentions the things that she gathered. As your child reads her poem aloud, she can use the objects as props.

Mastery occurs when: your child can use the list of information to create her own free verse poetry.

You may want to help your child a little more if: she is having trouble getting started. You may want to write a poem as an example.

7 | Tall and Slouchy Nouns

TIME: 15 minutes

MATERIALS
- list of common and proper nouns
- chair

Learning happens when: you talk about common and proper nouns with your child, who is sitting on the chair. A noun names a person, place, thing, idea, quality, or act. A common noun names any one of a group—not a specific person, place, thing, quality, or act. A common noun is *not* capitalized. A proper noun names a specific person, place, thing, idea, quality, or act. A proper noun *is* capitalized.

Common Nouns	Proper Nouns
man	Mr. Cowan
book	*Harry Potter and the Sorcerer's Stone*
dog	Fido

Ask your child to tell you in his own words what a common noun is. How is it different from a proper noun? Which words start with a capital letter? Explain that you will read a word. If the word is a common noun, your child will slouch in his seat to show that it starts with a lowercase letter. If the word is a proper noun, your child will sit up very tall in the chair to show that the word starts with an uppercase letter.

- Listening and responding to information is right up your auditory learner's alley, but you can strengthen this connection by asking your child to say "proper noun" every time he sits up very tall, signifying that the word is a proper noun.

- If you have a visual learner, you may want to write out the words on a board as you say them. Or, you can ask your child to write the word after he sits or slouches.

- Make this game a little more active for your kinesthetic learner by asking him to jump straight up in the air for a proper noun and sit cross-legged on the ground for common nouns.

Mastery occurs when: your child can identify and differentiate between proper and common nouns.

You may want to help your child a little more if: he is mixing up the proper and common nouns. Before your child moves in the seat, review the difference between common and proper nouns.

8 Dice-y Writing

TIME: 30 minutes

MATERIALS

pair of dice

paper

pencils

Learning happens when: you talk to your child about ways to write a story. What parts make up a story? How do you write a story? Offer to help your child write a story in a fun way. Your child can use the dice as a way to structure her writing. To create the title of the story, ask your child to roll the dice. The number shown on the dice equals the number of words to be used in the title. The next roll shows the number of words your child should write to begin the story. Continue rolling the dice and writing down words until your child has created a story. Using a specific number of words helps your child focus more on the words she selects.

Variations: Join in. Take turns rolling the dice and adding to the story. You could make it go in a totally different direction with just a few words.

- Talk this activity out with your child before she writes. Sometimes auditory learners need to vocalize the words before writing them down.

- Ask your child to create an illustration that corresponds to some of the sentences that she has written.

- Rolling the dice and writing words that match the numbers involve movement with writing. Add to the movement of the activity by writing the story on big paper or a whiteboard that is hung on the wall.

Mastery occurs when: your child can convey her thoughts onto paper under specific constraints.

You may want to help your child a little more if: she is having difficulty sticking to the number of words. Remind your child that the roll of the dice is just the number of words; they don't have to be complete sentences. If it proves to be a major stumbling block, add another die into the mix to increase the number of words your child can use.

9 | Creepy Books

TIME: 45 minutes

Learning happens when: you and your child trace circles onto the construction paper and cut them out. As you work, ask your child to describe what happens in a story he has recently read. Who is in the story? Where does the story take place? What is the first major event? What is the next? How does it end? If there was a problem or obstacle, was it overcome? Have your child choose one of the cut-out circles to be a caterpillar's head. Let your child decorate the face however he chooses. Write the main character's name on another colored circle and have your child draw the character on it. Do this for all of the characters, then move on to the settings. From here, your child will describe the major events of the story, drawing pictures in each circle. When your child completes the story, he can decorate a tail piece. Using the hole punch and string, connect all the circles in order to create a creepy caterpillar of a tale!

MATERIALS
- circle tracer (a mug, a bowl, or a coaster)
- construction paper in many colors
- pencils, crayons, and markers
- rounded-edge scissors
- recently read book
- hole punch
- string

- After you've finished putting together the caterpillar, ask your child to tell you the story.

- Instead of having you write everything, ask your little visual learner to help you. Even if he can't spell the name of a particular character, your child can always look it up in the book.

✍ Make a modified version. When your child finishes reading a book, instead of including all the details, have him make a face and just one circle. Have your child write the title and the author of the book and draw an illustration on the circle. For each book your child reads, add another body part (circle) with the title, the author, and an illustration.

Mastery occurs when: your child can pick out the major parts of the story and write about them.

You may want to help your child a little more if: he is mixing up the order of the story. Start with an easier book, or let your child use the book to check his work.

10 An Interview with a Monster

TIME: 30–45 minutes

MATERIALS
□ unlined paper
□ crayons or markers
□ lined paper
□ pencils

Learning happens when: you ask your child to draw a picture of a monster. Your child can make it look however she wants and name it whatever she likes. Explain to your child that she will be interviewing the monster. Make a list of questions with her to ask the monster that start with: who, what, where, when, why, and how. Some good examples:

When were you born?

Where were you born?

What is your favorite color?

How many brothers and sisters do you have?

Why do you live under the couch?

After you and your child have made your list of questions, help her to set up a format for an interview like this one:

Title: An Interview with [monster's name]

By: [your child's name]

Child:

Monster:

Child:

Monster:

Ask your child to fill in the list of questions after the line labeled "Child." Point out that the writing is in the second person (you, your). Then, let your child fill in the monster's responses. Make sure that she is writing in the first person (I, me). When your child is finished, let her reread the interview and check for mistakes.

Variations: Ask your child to write the questions and you come up with the answers.

- After editing any mistakes, read the interview aloud with your child.

- Ask your child to underline all the pronouns that she can find in the interview. Use different colors for different words or use different colors for your child's lines and those of the monster.

- Don't just read it, do it! Ask another family member or a friend to videotape the interview between your child and the monster (you). Play it back so your child can watch.

Mastery occurs when: your child can write in an interview format, switching from second person to first person.

You may want to help your child a little more if: she has difficulty remembering which pronouns to use. Let your child say the question to you and then write it down. Do the same for the answers. You can also use a magazine as an example if your child is having difficulty with the format.

11 Sentence Book

TIME: 30–45 minutes

MATERIALS
white paper
crayons or markers
pencils
stapler

Learning happens when: your child takes two sheets of white paper and folds them in half to create eight book pages. Open the book and staple it in the middle.

On the first page ask your child to write the following: "My Four Kinds of Sentences Book."

On the second page: "Author and Illustrator: [your child's name]."

On the third page: "There are four kinds of sentences."

On the fourth page: "Declarative sentences make a statement." Then ask your child to write an example and illustrate it.

On the fifth page: "Imperative sentences make a command." Let your child write another sentence as an example and illustrate it.

On the sixth page: "Exclamatory sentences show a strong feeling." Your child then writes an example of an exclamatory sentence and draws a picture to go with it.

On the seventh page: "Interrogative sentences ask a question." Your child writes an example and draws a picture to illustrate the sentence.

On the eighth page: "The End."

Read through your child's book with him.

Variations: Write another book, but make this one for parts of speech. Follow the same directions that you used for the types of sentences book. On page three ask your child to write "This Is My Parts of Speech Book" and the page that follows may contain a part of speech.

⟁ After your child has created the book, ask him to explain what each type of sentence is and exactly how the illustration is an example.

👁 Ask your child to illustrate each part of speech in more than one way.

✋ Instead of drawing an illustration, ask your kinesthetic learner to act out each type of sentence for you.

Mastery occurs when: your child can write examples of each of the four sentence types correctly.

You may want to help your child a little more if: he is getting the four sentence types confused. Read some books with your child and ask him to pick out the different types of sentences. Review them as your child finds them.

12 Literature Response Journal

TIME: 20–30 minutes

MATERIALS
- pencils
- lined paper
- hole punch
- three-ring binder

Learning happens when: you and your child put together a literature response journal. After your child finishes reading a book, have her write about it in the journal. Ask your child to write about what she liked or didn't like about the book. Your child should write about the characters and how they relate to her. Ask her to write about what new information she learned from the book and what else she would like to know.

Variations: Extend your child's writing by researching something she found in the story. If it was a book about types of cats, look up information about one that caught her interest. Where are they found? What do they eat? How do they live? Ask your child to write the new information in the journal.

🦻 If your child is an auditory learner, try this activity on tape first. Then, ask your child to use the tape to help write in her journal.

👁 This is a great activity just the way it is if your child is a visual learner, but you can reinforce the concepts by asking her to illustrate the journal.

✋ Ask your child to cut out pictures from old magazines to add to her journal.

Mastery occurs when: your child can write her opinions and conclusions freely in the journal.

You may want to help your child a little more if: she is having trouble getting started. You might want to set up a form for your child to use at first. Draw a line where your child can write the title. Draw new lines for the author, the setting, the characters, major events, likes, and dislikes. Make the pages look like a form that she can fill out. Leave enough space for your child to elaborate once the juices get flowing.

Spelling

Children in the second grade are learning how to include a lot of new things into their writing, and they will need to add more difficult spelling and vocabulary words into the mix. The days of c-a-t are over. In second grade c-a-t becomes p-a-n-t-h-e-r, and a whole lot of other simple words will become more complex, in both meaning and spelling.

Spelling is based on letter sounds and the order in which letters form words. Sound like phonics? Your child already spells phonetically—and this skill will be useful for a lifetime, but phonetic spelling is not always correct. As the words are starting to get more difficult, so are the ways to spell them. There are silent vowels, blends, and letters that don't look the way they are supposed to sound. Second graders will be learning these new rules for spelling. With a little more practice and some help from you, your child will be able to spell an even larger number of words from memory.

The following table describes some of the important skills related to spelling and vocabulary, where children can run into problems, and what you can do to help them along.

Spelling Skills	Having Problems?	Quick Tips
Is able to spell sight words from memory.	Has difficulty spelling from memory.	Flash cards are a simple way to help your child drill the more simple sight words.
Can sound out and spell new words with relative success.	Cannot sound out or spell new words.	Start with smaller words. Try to have your child locate smaller words in the larger words, or try rhyming or beats to give a rhythm to the word.

Spelling Activities

 Sidewalk Spelling

Learning happens when: you and your child take the learning outside. Have your child practice writing the words on the sidewalk. Have him write them in a pattern, then shout the words out while jumping to the word you say. Have your child spell the word as he jumps on it, or say the words while he jumps on them.

Variations: Make the words in the snow! Mix food coloring with water in a spray bottle, bundle up with your child, and start spraying words in the snow.

TIME: 20 minutes

MATERIALS
- list of words (either your child's school spelling list or a list of words that are a challenge for your child)
- colored chalk

📖 Have your child read the words aloud as he is writing them. Ask your child to say the words while jumping on them.

👁 Let your child retrace what he has written in a different color of chalk.

✋ This is a great kinesthetic activity as it's written—get jumping!

Mastery occurs when: your child correctly spells the words from the list.

You may want to help your child a little more if: he is having difficulty spelling the words. Your child may first need to see the word. Write the words on index cards, or write them once on the sidewalk then let your child repeat them a few times.

2 Spelling Hangman

TIME: 5–20 minutes

MATERIALS
▪ chalkboard or whiteboard
▪ chalk or whiteboard marker
▪ list of words (either your child's school spelling list or a list of words that are a challenge for your child)

Set up the hangman game on the board by making an upside-down *L*.

Learning happens when: you choose a word from the list and draw a line for each of the letters in the word on the board. Let your child take guesses at the letters in the word. If your child correctly guesses a letter in the word, write it down in the appropriate space. If your child chooses an incorrect letter, draw a person's head. Continue to fill in the letters in the word with each correct guess and to draw parts of a person's body—arms, legs, hands, and feet—for each incorrect letter. If your child thinks she knows the word, let her take a guess. Play a game of hangman for each word on the list.

Saying the letters aloud as you write them down is good for your child, but you can also ask her to use the word in a sentence or to define the word. If your child is struggling, you should use the word in a sentence or define it.

Let your child glance at the list of words prior to playing the game. If the game is still too hard, let your child glance at a few words, then try the game again using just those words.

Let your child write the letters in the proper spot and draw the hanged man.

Mastery occurs when: your child can correctly identify the words.

You may want to help your child a little more if: she is not able to figure out the words. Start with one or two letters already in the puzzle, especially lesser-used letters. You can also have your child make an alphabet line to cross off letters that are wrong guesses.

3 | Spelling and Vocabulary Concentration

Cut the index cards into fourths. Write each word from the list on half of the little cards. Write the definition for each word on the remaining cards.

Learning happens when: you mix up the cards and spread them out face down on a tabletop in front of your child. Ask your child to choose a card. If the card is a word, have him say the word, spell it, and define it. Then have your child choose another card, searching for the definition. If your child chooses a card with a definition, have him come up with a word that matches the definition. Continue until your child has matched all the cards.

TIME: 30 minutes

MATERIALS
- index cards
- rounded-edge scissors
- markers
- list of words (either your child's school spelling list or a list of words that are a challenge for your child)

Variations: Use all definitions or all words. Let your child find the matches on sheets of paper, one listing the words, the other listing the definitions.

⟨⟩ Instead of matching the words to definitions on the cards, draw pictures on one side of the card. Let your child look at the picture side of the cards while you say a definition. Ask him to pick out the picture that matches the definition that you say.

👁 Ask your child to help you create all the cards. This will help familiarize your visual learner with the words, spelling, and definitions.

✋ Try using action words, such as "hop" or "jump." Ask your child to act out the word before locating the definition.

Mastery occurs when: your child can correctly spell words and associate them with the definitions.

You may want to help your child a little more if: he is confusing the words and the definitions. Start off with a smaller list of words and gradually add in a few more words.

4   Heads Up

Learning happens when: you write all of the words on the board. Let your child study the words for a while. Ask her to put her head down. Erase one of the words. Let your child study the words again. Have her guess the word that's missing and then spell it. Continue until all the words have been erased. As the words dwindle, it's okay to give hints if your child is struggling to remember what's already been used.

👂 Ask your child to locate the word that's missing, use it in a sentence, and then spell it.

👁 This activity is already suited to your visual learner, but you can reinforce the activity by letting your child write in the word that is missing.

✋ Use words that represent objects around your house. Ask your child to find the object that represents the missing word.

Mastery occurs when: your child can choose the missing word and spell it correctly.

You may want to help your child a little more if: she is getting confused over which words are missing. This activity is not only an exercise in spelling, but in memory as well. Try it with half the words, or give your child a cheat sheet to look at.

TIME: 20 minutes

MATERIALS
■ chalkboard or white-board
■ chalk or whiteboard marker
■ board eraser
■ list of words (either your child's school spelling list or a list of words that are a challenge to your child)

5 | Spelling Story Starters

Learning happens when: you write a few story starters at the top of a piece of paper. These are some ideas:

- Once upon a time, there was an evil wizard who . . .

- "Stop!" Everyone turned to look at . . .

- The woman in the red dress walked through the store hoping to find the perfect . . .

TIME: 30 minutes

MATERIALS
■ paper
■ pencils
■ list of words (either your child's school spelling list or a list of words that are a challenge for your child)

The starter just needs to be something that your child can elaborate on. Let him choose a starter that interests him and write it at the top of a clean sheet of paper. Then have him continue the story using each spelling word in a sentence. Read the finished story together and have your child check for any mistakes. After he edits it, hang up the finished story.

Variations: Write a poem instead of a story. Remind your child that a poem does not have to rhyme. Many children read Dr. Seuss and think that's the only way to write a poem. A poem especially effective if the word list has words that are related to each other, such as words from a project your child is working on at school.

👂 Ask your child to read the story to a younger sibling or other family member.

👁 Ask your child to illustrate the main parts of the story.

✋ Help your child act out the story when he is finished.

Mastery occurs when: your child correctly spells the words and uses them in sentences to create a story.

You may want to help your child a little more if: he is having difficulty continuing the story. You may want to choose a few words to have your child incorporate throughout the story, as opposed to including one in each sentence. Once your child is comfortable, have him add a few more words.

6 Spelling with Pipe Cleaners

TIME: 30 minutes

MATERIALS
▪ large assortment of pipe cleaners
▪ list of words (either your child's school spelling list or a list of words that are a challenge for your child)

Learning happens when: you have your child use pipe cleaners to spell out the words on the list. It allows your child to focus on each individual letter while creating the word.

Variations: Use Wikki Stix, pretzel shapes, pasta, or Play-doh to spell out the words. This activity can be adapted to whatever you have on hand or whatever makes your child excited to work.

✋ Ask your child to spell the word aloud after creating the word with the pipe cleaner letters.

👁 If your child is a visual learner, ask her to write the word after she has made the letters with the pipe cleaners.

👂 This gives your child a chance to physically form the letters, which is great for kinesthetic learners.

Mastery occurs when: your child can correctly create the letters and spell the words.

You may want to help your child a little more if: she is having trouble forming the letters to make the words. Use shaving foam or whipped cream and let your child use her fingers as the writing tool.

7 Spelling Rhymes

Learning happens when: you and your child sing the following song together, using your child's name. Let's use "Drew" as the first example:

TIME: 5–20 minutes

MATERIALS
list of words (either your child's school spelling list or a list of words that are a challenge for your child)

Drew, Drew, bo boo,

Bananafana mo moo,

Me, mi, mo moo, Drew.

Here's another example with Sarah:

Sarah, Sarah, bo bara,

Bananafana mo mara,

Me, mi, mo mara, Sarah.

Once your child has the song down, try it with the words on the word list. Sing through the song and then ask your child to spell the word. The rhythmic pattern of the song helps your child internalize the word, while spelling it helps reinforce the word.

Choose any song that has a lot of repetition or repetitive rhythm in it. Another good one to use is "What's My Name?" from the Disney *Silly Songs* album.

Get a photocopy of the song you're using so your visual learner can follow along, or help your child write out the words on a whiteboard or a chalkboard.

Clap, stomp, jump, or whatever you can think of to make the song rhythmic as well!

Mastery occurs when: your child can correctly spell the words on the list.

You may want to help your child a little more if: he is having problems remembering the rhyme. Simplify it to a beat—hand clapping or foot stomping with each letter.

8 | "I'm the Teacher!"

TIME: 20 minutes

MATERIALS

- paper
- pencils
- list of words (either your child's school spelling list or a list of words that are a challenge for your child)

Learning happens when: your child becomes the teacher. Let your child give *you* the spelling test. Ask her to read each word on the list to you and then you write it down. Make some mistakes for your little teacher to find. After you are finished, give your child the test to correct. Ask her to give you a grade.

Ask your child to help you spell each word to check your work. Read a word off your test and then ask her to spell it for you.

Make up your own list of words, using more difficult words. Have your child read you those instead. Using bigger words will introduce your child to new vocabulary. Ask her to look up the words in the dictionary for meanings.

Ask your child to write each word out on a whiteboard or a chalkboard so that you can check your own work.

Mastery occurs when: your child can correctly identify any errors you made and correct them.

You may want to help your child a little more if: she is having difficulty noticing the mistakes you've made. Let your child match your test to the list to search for mistakes.

9 Scrambled Letters

Learning happens when: you sit with your child and cut out various letters from magazines and newspapers. Scramble the letters, then let your child pick out the letters that spell each word on the list. Ask your child to glue each letter to the paper to create the word. Complete the spelling list and then read through and spell the words with your child.

> TIME: 30 minutes
>
> MATERIALS
> - magazines
> - newspapers
> - rounded-edge scissors
> - paper
> - glue
> - list of words (either your child's school spelling list or a list of words that are a challenge for your child)

Talk with your child about the letters that create blends in words. Ask him to say the words that have blends such as *sh* or *ch* in them.

This activity is great for visual learners just as it is.

Ask your child to create the letters with his body. Use a Polaroid or digital camera to take photos of your child as each letter of the alphabet (as best he can—feel free to use props) and use those photos to create words. A digital camera is great for this because it's easy to create many copies of frequently used letters.

Mastery occurs when: your child can spell each word correctly.

You may want to help your child a little more if: he is having diffi-culty spelling the words. Use only a few different large-size fonts. You could even print them off the computer. Sometimes, too many sizes and shapes can confuse your child.

Environmental Learning

Your child has *tons* of opportunities to practice his or her new writing skills in day-to-day activities. Get your child a journal or diary to write down interesting or private notes. Ask your child to write out his or her own thank-you notes for gifts, and letters or postcards to cousins or close relatives.

What will help your child extend his or her newly found writing skills is practice and copying. Reading new things and trying to emu-late the style of the writing is one way for your child to practice new skills. Let him help you write lists and notes. Help your child make spe-cial stationery just for his letters.

Don't forget that the easiest way for your child to copy writing style is by copying yours. Let your child observe you reading and writing every day. The more immersed your child is in reading and writing, the easier and more fun it will be.

End of Second Grade Writing Checklist

Students who are working at the standard level at the end of second grade:

____ Write about their own ideas

____ Pick out nouns and verbs in sentences

____ Explain the problem, solution, or main idea in fiction and nonfiction

____ Revise their writing to make it clearer

____ Read and understand stories, poems, plays, directories, newspapers, charts, and diagrams

____ Write different types of sentences

Second Grade Math 7

S econd grade math starts with a review of the basics from first grade and then moves to a series of new skills. Your budding mathematician will learn to order, label, and express quantities to solve problems. He or she will also begin to convert language into mathematical problems—understanding the math of everyday life while getting a little more formal with the way he or she expresses math problems. Pretty soon "take away" becomes minus and subtraction. Suddenly a simple "and" between phrases can make it an addition problem. Soon fractions become a part of your child's math world, as do patterns and spatial relationships. That's a lot, but don't worry, your child is ready for it!

Beginning of Second Grade Math Checklist

Students who are working at the standard level at the beginning of second grade:

____ Work with patterns and sequences

____ Add and subtract single and two-digit numbers

____ Tell time by hours and minutes

____ Estimate and predict simple outcomes

____ Count money

____ Identify place values to hundreds

____ Practice measuring length, capacity, and weight

____ Work with geometric shapes

____ Become familiar with the concept of symmetry

____ Count higher than 100

____ Identify the fractions $1/2$, $1/3$, and $1/4$

____ Solve simple word problems

Addition and Subtraction

Addition and subtraction are mathematical operations that second graders begin to explore in more depth. They will be moving beyond one-digit operations and starting to add and subtract with two- and sometimes three-digit numbers. Of course, along with adding two-digit numbers comes carrying numbers, which can be tricky! As well as adding and subtracting, your child will be manipulating money. Second graders will learn how much money is worth, how much things cost, and how much they might have versus the price of whatever it is they want. Maybe it will calm the "I wants" at the toy store if you ask your child to look at the price! Addition and subtraction are part of the essential math skills your child will need to move on to multiplication and division in the upcoming years.

The following table describes some important skills related to addition and subtraction, where children can run into problems, and what you can do to help them along.

Addition and Subtraction Skills	Having Problems?	Quick Tips
Understands the relationship between addition and subtraction to solve problems and check solutions.	Does not understand how to check work with reverse operation.	Create fact families: $1+2=3 \quad 2+1=3$ $3-1=2 \quad 3-2=1$ to show the relationship between addition and subtraction.
Finds the sum or difference of two whole numbers with up to three digits.	Cannot add or subtract large numbers.	Have your child "help" you with the bills or your checkbook.
Reads and writes whole numbers and identifies the place value for each digit.	Has difficulty reading or writing numbers, and cannot identify place values easily.	Use flash cards. I know, flash cards are so boring, but the repetition *does* help your child learn the numbers and place values.
Explores combinations of coins (penny, nickel, dime, quarter, $1/2$ dollar).	Confuses the amount each coin or group of coins is worth.	Start an at-home savings account. Give your child ten pennies a few times a week and let him or her exchange them for other denominations
Uses mental arithmetic to find the sum or difference of numbers.	Has trouble adding or subtracting numbers in his or her head.	Quiz your child, but relate it to daily life; say, "I have three potatoes and this recipe calls for five. How many more do I need?"

Addition and Subtraction Activities

1 Ten Rings

Learning happens when: you give your child a plastic bag filled with cereal. Ask your child to take out pieces of cereal and start grouping them into piles of ten. While he is doing that, cut pipe cleaners in half and give your child ten pieces. Let your child put ten pieces of cereal on each pipe cleaner and then bend the ends to hold the pieces on. Using the pipe cleaners as visual tools, ask your child to add the following:

TIME: 15 minutes

MATERIALS
zip-top plastic bag
breakfast cereal with a hole in the middle
pipe cleaners

10 + 30	40 + 50	20 + 50
20 + 60	80 + 10	40 + 30
70 + 20	90 + 10	70 + 10

Your child should be able figure out the sums using the pipe cleaners.

Variations: Use rings of five instead of ten. Then your child can add more numbers or pair them up to use as rings of ten.

- 👂 Ask your child to skip count (count by 2s, 5s, or 10s) aloud while grouping the pipe cleaners.

- 👁 If your visual learner needs more reinforcement, try drawing a shape on paper for each of the groups of cereal and ask your child to place the groups in the shapes that you have drawn.

- ✋ Making the pipe cleaners and grouping them is great for kinesthetic learners as is.

Mastery occurs when: your child can answer the problem using the cereal as visual help.

You may want to help your child a little more if: he is having trouble coming up with the correct sum. Although the basis for this activity is to get your child used to adding by tens, to answer each problem he may need to count out each piece of cereal individually and then make a loop.

2 Place Values

TIME: 15–20 minutes

MATERIALS
- pencils
- paper
- gumdrops
- toothpicks
- breakfast cereal with a hole in the middle

Learning happens when: you and your child discuss what place values are. What is the difference between 5, 50, and 500? Ask your child to divide the paper into three columns. The left-hand column represents the hundreds place, the middle column the tens place, and the right-hand column the ones place. Place one gumdrop in each column. Put a toothpick through the center of each gumdrop (you may need to cut the gumdrop in half prior to starting the activity). Give your child a handful of the cereal. Using 19 as an example, ask your child how she could use the cereal to represent that amount by placing the cereal on the toothpicks. What number is in the ones place? What number is in the tens place? On the middle toothpick, put one piece of cereal. On the right toothpick put nine pieces. Try a few more two-digit numbers and then add in three-digit numbers. You and your child can do this for any number up to 999!

 Associate a sound with each place value. Ask your child to snap her fingers the same number of times as there are numbers in the ones place, to clap for the number of tens, and to tap for the number of hundreds. (The number 375 would be 3 taps, 7 claps, and 5 snaps.)

👁 Ask your child to write the place value by writing the ones in the "ones" column, the tens in the "tens" column, and the hundreds in the "hundreds" column.

✋ This activity is good for kinesthetic learners as written; placing the cereal rings on the proper toothpick to show the place value of the number you say incorporates movement with learning. You can add to this by asking your child to hop in place the same number of times as there are numbers in the ones place, turn circles for the number of tens, and do jumping jacks that equal the number of hundreds (for example, the number 375 would be 3 jumping jacks, 7 circles, and 5 hops).

Mastery occurs when: your child can accurately represent the numbers using the cereal and toothpicks.

You may want to help your child a little more if: she is confusing the place values. Try the same activity but this time use numbers that are just represented by one column (500, 40, 3). Work up to numbers that use two columns (540) and then get to numbers that use all three columns (543).

❘3❘ Missing Numbers

Learning happens when: you and your child create math sentences (equations). Ask your child how he would write "Five plus what equals seven?" Let your child write out that sentence. It should look like this: $5 + \_\_\_ = 7$. Try another sentence with your child. Then read the following sentences to your child and have him write each of them down:

Time: 20 minutes

Materials
▪ paper
▪ pencils

$$6 - \underline{\quad} = 2 \qquad \underline{\quad} + 9 = 0$$

$$\underline{\quad} + 12 = 15 \qquad 13 - 4 = \underline{\quad}$$

$$28 - \underline{\quad} = 14 \qquad 55 + \underline{\quad} = 75$$

$$17 - \underline{\quad} = 4 \qquad \underline{\quad} + 64 + 4 = 70$$

$$\underline{\quad} + \underline{\quad} = 11 \qquad 36 - \underline{\quad} = 24$$

Variations: Read each sentence to your child and help him write it out. Then, have your child solve the problem. Ask your child to create some of his own math sentences to figure out.

- If your child is able, ask him to write down the sentence and then share the answer aloud. This is an advanced skill, so you may want to make the sentences a little simpler for him.

- Ask your child to read each sentence to you and help him write it out. Then, have your child solve the problem. Ask your child to create some of his own math sentences to figure out.

- Give your child small items to use in figuring out the answers to the math sentences.

Mastery occurs when: your child can relate the word sentences to numbers to complete the missing digit.

You may want to help your child a little more if: he is having difficulty writing the sentence. Write out the sentence in number form on an index card and use it as a flash card. Ask your child to give it a few tries and if he is still having difficulty, flash the card as a hint.

4 | Mental Math

TIME: 30 minutes

MATERIALS
- pencils
- graph paper with 50 large squares (you can print some at www.knowledgeessentials.com)
- rounded-edge scissors
- blank paper
- bowl or box
- calculator

Learning happens when: your child writes whatever numbers from 1 to 99 she wants in the 50 boxes on the graph paper. Ask your child to cut out each number square and put it in the bowl or box. Explain to your child that she will choose two numbers, and while you are adding them in your head, she will be adding them on the paper to check you. Let your child choose two of the number squares from the box and read them aloud. While you try to do the mental math, your child should write the problem out and add it up. Say your answer, compare it to your child's answer, and then have your child check the answer using the calculator.

- 👂 If your child is good at mental math, switch roles and have her try to come up with the answer while you write it out. Or use subtraction instead of addition, putting the bigger number first.

- 👁 This activity is great for visual learners as is.

- ✋ Let your kinesthetic learner use her pipe cleaner cereal groups (see activity 1 in this section) to represent the numbers that she is trying to add.

Mastery occurs when: your child can add the two numbers correctly.

You may want to help your child a little more if: she is having trouble adding up the two-digit numbers. Start with the numbers 1 to 25 and use fewer boxes. Gradually increase the numbers as your child gets more comfortable.

5 Cross

TIME: 30 minutes

MATERIALS

- paper
- pencils
- spinner from 0 to 9 (tape paper to the bottom of a spinner in one of your child's board games and write the numbers from 0 to 9 on it)

Print record sheets that look like the ones shown. (You can find them at www.knowlegeessentials.com). You can also re-create this page by drawing the shapes on big paper.

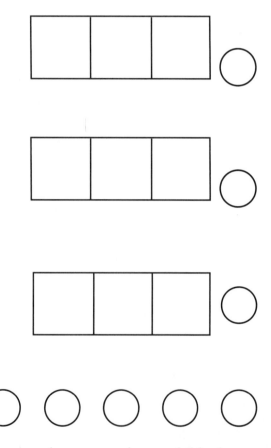

Learning happens when: you and your child take turns spinning the spinner. Have your child put each number that he spins into any one of the nine squares on the sheet while you write the numbers you spin on another sheet. Continue taking turns until all of the squares are filled. Ask your child to add up the rows from left to right and put the answer in the circle while you do the same to your sheet. Then ask your child to start adding the columns from top to bottom and put the answers in the corresponding circles. Lastly, ask your child to add the two diagonal rows and put the answers in the circles.

After you have both filled in the circles, take a look at the numbers in the circles. Any sum that appears only once should be crossed out. Add up the remaining sums to get the score for that round. Play a few rounds to see who has the highest score—he is the Cross king!

Variations: Change the spinner to include two-digit numbers from 10 to 19. As your child gets more skilled at adding those two-digit numbers, use larger numbers.

- Ask your child to say the numbers and add them aloud. Discuss with your child ways to get a score of zero using numbers 0 to 9.

- The visual images created by this activity are very appealing to visual learners. Try letting your child make his own record sheet but in a different shape or pattern.

- Spinning is lots of fun for your child, and you can add more movement to the activity by letting him use marbles or other objects to hold and count.

Mastery occurs when: your child can add the numbers in the rows, columns, and diagonals correctly.

You may want to help your child a little more if: he has difficulty adding the numbers correctly. Start with adding just the rows. Some children have issues visually adding any other way. Ask your child to try the columns and practice until he is more confident. Then move on to the diagonals. If need be, let your child rewrite the numbers to add outside of the box.

6 Addition Bingo

TIME: 20 minutes

MATERIALS
- markers
- paper
- index cards
- pencils

Draw two grids four squares across and four squares down or print two copies of the one you find at www.knowledgeessentials. com. Fill in each square on the grids with any number from 0 to 18 (making sure the grids are different). Make two sets of index cards numbered 0 to 9 and separate them into two piles.

Learning happens when: you give your child one grid and keep the other one. Ask your child to choose a card from each pile and add the two numbers together. If that number appears on her grid, ask her to cross it off. Then you choose two numbers, add them, and check to see if it's on your grid. If so, cross it off. This continues until you or your child has either a row of 4, a column of 4, a diagonal of 4, or the 4 corners crossed off.

Variations: You can do this with subtraction as well. Subtract the smaller number from the larger number. This will change the numbers that your child can choose for her grid. With subtraction, the largest number will be only 9 and the smallest will be 0.

👂 Add or subtract aloud.

👁 Let your child use scrap paper to add or subtract by writing.

✋ Give your child objects to represent the numbers that she is trying to add or subtract.

Mastery occurs when: your child can add two numbers together correctly.

You may want to help your child a little more if: she is having problems adding up the numbers. Use small objects to help your child physically manipulate the numbers.

7 | Subtraction War

Learning happens when: you and your child sit down to play the card game War with a new set of rules. Take out the face cards and make the aces equal to one. To play, ask your child to split the remaining cards evenly between the two of you. Next, you and your child should each flip over two cards from the top of your pile at the same time. Then you each subtract the smaller number from the larger number shown on the cards. The person with the largest answer wins all four cards. If someone gives an incorrect answer, the other person has to correctly subtract the two numbers to win all the cards. Continue until someone wins all the cards.

TIME: 20 minutes

MATERIALS
- deck of cards

Variations: Try this game with addition. To make the game more advanced, give the face cards numerical value ($J = 11, Q = 12$, and $K = 13$).

- 👂 You and your child say the numbers on the cards aloud, say the subtraction problem that they make aloud, and say the answer aloud.

- 👁 Ask your child to create his own cards. This is a great way to get your visual learner motivated!

- ✋ Flipping cards will keep your child engaged, but if he is struggling try adding or subtracting real objects that represent the numbers on the cards.

Mastery occurs when: your child can subtract the two numbers correctly in a relatively short amount of time.

You may want to help your child a little more if: he is having difficulty subtracting the numbers quickly. Flash cards are a big help in getting your child to answer simple subtraction problems with more ease. Quiz your child with some flash cards before playing the game to boost his confidence.

8 | Twenty-One

TIME: 20 minutes

MATERIALS
- paper
- pencils
- sugar cube
- markers

Learning happens when: you ask your child to write the number 21 at the top of a sheet of paper and the numbers 1, 2, and 3 on the sugar cube to make a die. The rules of this game are simple. You and your child take turns rolling the die and subtracting 1, 2, or 3 from 21. Continue to take turns rolling the die and subtracting 1, 2, or 3 from the previous answer. If the die lands on a blank side you miss a turn. The person who reaches zero first wins. You can speed up the game by filling in all the sides of the die.

Variations: Go backward. Start at zero and add 1, 2, or 3. The first person to reach 21 wins. Try it with other numbers—your child's birthdate, for example.

- Ask your child to say each problem aloud to you, such as "21 minus 3 equals 18" and "18 minus 1 equals 17."
- This activity is great for visual learners as is.
- Rolling the die will keep your child engaged, but if she is struggling, try starting with a pile of 21 objects and let your child take away 1, 2, or 3 as warranted.

Mastery occurs when: your child correctly subtracts the numbers from 21 down to zero.

You may want to help your child a little more if: she has trouble subtracting the numbers. Start with a smaller number, such as 10, and use only 1 and 2 as options. When your child has mastered this, start using a larger number and more subtraction number choices.

9 Envelopes of Money

Make value envelopes before sitting down with your child. On each envelope, write down an amount, such as $0.46. Put these aside.

TIME: 20 minutes

MATERIALS
- envelopes
- markers
- a lot of change

Learning happens when: you dump out a large amount of change in front of your child and let him sift through it. How much is each coin worth? What coin has the greatest value? The least value? How much money would your child have if he had one penny, one nickel, one dime, and one quarter?

Take out the envelopes and show them to your child. Ask him to select one and then use the pennies, nickels, dimes, and quarters to put the specific amount of money in the envelope. Check your child's change, and if applicable, have him find another way to achieve that amount.

Variations: Ask your child to find as many ways as possible to make the specified amount. There should be many ways to achieve each amount.

- The next time you see something that's labeled with a small amount, ask your child what coins would make up that amount.

- This activity is already geared toward your visual learner—use it as is.

- Go to a store with your child and a container of change. Look at the prices of various small items that are under a dollar. Give your child a dollar in pennies and ask how many he would need for a certain item. Try it with nickels, dimes, and quarters, then mix it up with different denominations.

Mastery occurs when: your child understands how different combinations of coins can equal a specific amount.

You may want to help your child a little more if: he is having trouble coming up with the coins that equal the specified amount. Go back to the basics—discuss how much each coin is worth. Then go over how many pennies are in a nickel, how many nickels are in a dime, and so on. Try again, starting with the easier envelopes first.

10 Grocery Shopping

TIME: 30 minutes

MATERIALS
- grocery store circular
- grocery list containing 5–10 items based on the circular
- coupons
- pencils
- paper
- rounded-edge scissors

Learning happens when: you and your child talk about grocery shopping. Ask your child to help you find out how much money you will need to bring with you to the grocery store to buy the things on your list. Give your child the coupons and the circular. Read off an item from your list and have your child locate it in the circular. Ask your child to write down the item and its price on a sheet of paper. Read off another item. Ask your child to write down the item and the price and add the two prices together to get the running total. Continue until all the items on the list have a price. Then go through the coupons, subtracting the savings for each coupon. When your child is finished, go through the list together and double check. Add the discounted prices up. Now you're ready to go shopping! Take your child with you to the store when you do your shopping with that shopping list. Ask your child to pick out the things that you wrote on your list. Also point out the difference in prices between the name-brand items and the store brand. Ask your child if she knows why there's a difference and explain it to her if she doesn't.

👂 Talk with your child about smart spending habits. Why should you save money? What are some ways to save money?

👁 Choose a recipe with ingredients found in the circular. Ask your child to help you find the prices for the ingredients. Now, tell your child that you only have a certain amount of money to spend (such as $10). Can you buy all the ingredients?

✋ Ask your child to cut out pictures from the circular for as many items from the list as she can find. You can also let her organize the coupons.

Mastery occurs when: your child correctly finds the prices for the items, adds the prices together, and subtracts the discount amounts on the coupons.

You may want to help your child a little more if: all of the steps involved confuse your child. Rather than talking about all of the steps at the beginning of the activity, take one step at a time with your child. Talk about identifying the prices and do that. When your child is successful, say, "Now, let's see if we have any coupons for the items on the list." Write the discount beside the item price and place a subtraction sign between the price and the amount of the coupon. Applaud your child's success in setting up the problems. Work the subtraction problems with your child. Recognize her successfully solving them. Then help your child set up the addition problem. If she is having trouble adding more than two prices at a time, add the first two prices, then add their sum to the third price, adding its sum to the fourth price, and so on. The math isn't as hard as organizing the information in the activity. If you take the information in manageable chunks, you will greatly increase your child's ability to successfully complete the activity.

Shapes and Measurement

In first grade, children are introduced to measuring length, height, weight, and volume. They also start looking at time and temperature. Children are expected to learn and use the appropriate units of measure when solving problems dealing with measurement. But don't forget that there are also ways to measure things that don't use traditional units—with paper, fingers, desks, or feet. Anything that is not a normal way to measure is called nonstandard measurement, and it's something your child will be learning to do.

Shapes and Measurement Skills	Having Problems?	Quick Tips
Can see how measurement applies to everyday life.	Cannot relate standard and non-standard forms of measurement to real life.	Practice every day! Find how many footsteps it takes to go from the front door to the kitchen; have your child help you measure ingredients for meals.
Compares the concept of time and the passing of time using clocks and calendars.	Difficulty telling time or using a calendar.	Start a calendar with your child, adding in important dates and events. Break the calendar down to a weekly calendar, with time divisions on it. Write the week's activities down by the time associated with them.
Recognizes, identifies, and creates a circle, a quadrilateral, a rhombus, a square, a hexagon, a parallelogram, a trapezoid, and a triangle.	Confuses shapes.	Make it a game: while driving in the car or walking through a store, ask your child to find examples of a circle, a triangle, or a trapezoid.
Finds the perimeter of simple shapes	Does not grasp the concept of perimeter.	Let your child help you measure the rooms in your house to find the perimeter (you never know when you might want new carpets!).
Reads a thermometer.	Cannot read a thermometer.	Put up a thermometer outside your child's window and ask him or her every morning what the temperature is and what he or she should wear.

Second graders will be exploring shapes beyond circles, squares, and triangles. They will be learning about parallelograms, hexagons, trapezoids, and other less common shapes. Your child will learn to identify the similarities and differences between the shapes and how to find their perimeters and areas.

The table on page 112 describes some important skills related to shapes and measurement, where children can run into problems, and what you can do to help them along.

1 Hot or Cold?

Learning happens when: you ask your child to tell you which of the three bowls is filled with cold water. Which is hot? Which is warm? Ask your child if using his hand is a good idea for judging the temperature of water. Your child may answer that if the water is hot, it could burn—good thinking! But other than that, is using your hand a good indicator of the temperature of water?

Have your child put one hand in the hot water and one in the cold water and hold them there for a few seconds. Then, have him put both hands quickly in the warm water. Ask your child to concentrate on how each hand feels. Talk with your child about what the water felt like to both hands. Did one hand feel different from the other? How? Discuss the differences and ask if he still thinks that skin is a good sensor of temperature. Are there any other ways to reliably measure the temperature?

Discuss why a thermometer is a more reliable measure of temperature than our sense of touch. Let your child experiment with a thermometer. What will happen when it is put in hot water? In cold water?

Variations: Draw a few thermometers on a sheet of paper. Have one showing 85 degrees Fahrenheit, one showing 35 degrees

TIME: 10 minutes

MATERIALS
- one bowl each of hot (but not *too* hot), warm, and cold water
- towels
- thermometer
- paper
- crayons

Fahrenheit, and one showing 65 degrees Fahrenheit. Ask your child to write down if each temperature is hot, cold, or warm.

👂 What kind of sounds do you make when you are cold? What kind of sounds do you make when you are hot? Ask your child to make these sounds for you.

👁 Ask your child to illustrate the kind of clothing he would wear if the temperature were 95 degrees Fahrenheit. How about 20 degrees Fahrenheit? What about if it's 65 degrees Fahrenheit?

✋ This will appeal to your kinesthetic learner as is because he can feel the temperature that he is measuring.

Mastery occurs when: your child can identify different degrees of temperature on a thermometer.

You may want to help your child a little more if: he does not understand how to read the temperature from the thermometer.

2 Shadows

TIME: 20 minutes

MATERIALS
- chalk
- ruler
- pencils
- paper

Learning happens when: you ask your child what happens when she stands in the sun. Wait for a nice sunny day when you and your child have a lot of free time. Does she have a shadow? Is it tall? Is it short? How tall is her shadow in the morning? The afternoon? The evening? Ask your child to go out to the sidewalk early in the morning and stand in the sun. Draw a line with the chalk from her feet to the end of her shadow. Have her use the ruler to measure the length of the shadow (this will also have her using addition skills). Do this again at noon and in the early evening. At what time was the tallest shadow? What time was the shortest? What is the difference between the two?

Variations: Let your child draw your shadow as well and then compare the two. Subtract to find the differences in the lengths of the shadows.

- Talk with your child about shadows and why they change. How does the sun's movement change your shadow's size?

- After each measurement, ask your child to draw a picture of what her shadow looks like. Then ask her to put the hour underneath it.

- Ask your child to draw pictures that feature things such as a building, a tree, pets, and so forth, and their shadows.

Mastery occurs when: your child can accurately measure the length of the shadows and can subtract to find the differences.

You may want to help your child a little more if: she cannot measure the length correctly. Start off with something smaller. Put a stick in the ground and use that. Your child may also want to try using a measuring tape. This will let her focus on just the measuring.

3 Half Full

Pour ¼ cup of water in the first glass, ½ cup of water in the second glass, and ¾ cup of water in the third glass, and leave the last glass empty.

Learning happens when: you have your child examine the glasses. Which glass has the most water? Which glass has the least amount of water? Have your child estimate how many of the ¼ cups it would take to make 1 cup. Let your child check by using the measuring cup. Ask your child how many of the ½ cups it would take to fill 1 cup and then let him check.

TIME: 20 minutes

MATERIALS
- water
- measuring cup
- 4 identical glasses

Variations: Try this same activity using metric measurements.

🦻 Talk with your child about the different combinations of amounts you can make with the cups. Ask your child how many ¼ cups fit in the ¾ cup glass, or how many ½ cups fit into the ¾ cup glass.

👁 Try this activity again with different-shaped glasses, preferably ones that make less look like more and vice versa. Ask your child to estimate how much water he thinks might be in each glass. Have the measuring cup on hand for your child to use to check his guesses.

✋ Once your child gets the hang of estimating the amounts, use different types of materials, such as rice or gelatin.

Mastery occurs when: your child can estimate how many ¼ and ½ cups equal 1 cup.

You may want to help your child a little more if: he is estimating incorrectly. Use measuring cups instead of glasses. This will give your child a more visual representation of how much water is in 1 cup.

4 | I Measure Up!

TIME: 20–30 minutes

MATERIALS
- 8½ × 11-inch paper
- 12-inch ruler
- ball of string
- measuring tape
- rounded-edge scissors

Learning happens when: you and your child discuss how to measure things. What do you use to measure your height? A ruler? A tape measure? How about a piece of paper? Hand your child a piece of paper and ask her to use it to measure the length of the table. How many pieces of paper does it take?

Ask your child what she could use to measure her head. Can you use a ruler? Is it accurate? Suggest a piece of string.

Discuss how a string could help your child measure oddly shaped things. Give your child the ruler and the ball of string and ask her to measure the following body parts by first finding the length with the string and then measuring the string on the ruler:

Head	Shin	Upper arm
Wrist	Ring finger	Waist

- Ask your child to tell you about other things that can be used for nonstandard measurement. Try out a few of your child's suggestions and see how effective they are.

- If your child is a visual learner, try this: Use the ruler and string to measure your child's height, and cut the piece of string. Ask your child to paste the string to a long piece of paper and write the inches next to it. You can buy paper in a roll or you can make long paper by taping together short pieces of paper. A few months later, do it again. Compare the second piece of string to the first one and ask your child to figure out the difference.

- Your child will enjoy using the different objects to measure; this activity is good as is for kinesthetic learners.

Mastery occurs when: your child can measure various items using nonstandard measurement techniques.

You may want to help your child a little more if: the concept of non-standard measurement is confusing for your child.

5 | Ordering Time

Draw a clock face on each index card. Draw the hands on the clock, one for each hour of the day. Make sure to distinguish each hour with A.M. or P.M.

TIME: 15 minutes

MATERIALS
24 index cards
crayons or markers

Learning happens when: you mix up the cards and hand them to your child. Ask your child to put the cards in order starting at 12 A.M., or midnight. Go through the cards with your child to make sure she has them in order.

Variations: Once your child is comfortable with using the hour cards, start adding in half-hour, quarter-hour, and then various five-minute cards.

- Keep an eye on an analog clock or timepiece (not digital), one with minute and hour hands. When the clock hits the hour, ask your child what time it is. Try this in the morning when your child gets up, when she eats lunch, when she has a play date, or whenever there's going to be something happening on the hour, half hour, or other time increment.

- Choose a few cards for your child to illustrate. Have her use crayons and paper to draw what would be happening at say, 10:00 P.M.? How about 7:00 A.M.? 12:00 P.M.?

- Ask your child to use her arms to re-create the hour you're asking for. The little hand can be one arm held close to the body and bent at the elbow. The big hand is your child's other arm held straight.

Mastery occurs when: your child can correctly distinguish the order in which time progresses and what the difference is between A.M. and P.M.

You may want to help your child a little more if: she is confusing the time of day. The difference between A.M. and P.M. is easy to remember if you tell your child that *A* comes first in the alphabet and also begins the day, whereas *P* comes later in the alphabet and also later in the day.

7 Tangrams

Learning happens when: you and your child talk about shapes. What are some common shapes you see every day? The circle of a tire? The rectangular shape of a door? A square box? What are some uncommon shapes that are harder to find? A parallelogram? A trapezoid? Give your child a sheet of construction paper and a pair of scissors. Explain to your child that you will be making the pieces of a tangram puzzle now. A tangram is an ancient Chinese seven-piece puzzle, consisting of an assortment of triangles, squares, rectangles, trapezoids, and parallelograms. (You can see these shapes at www.knowledgeessentials.com.) The pieces are arranged to make dozens of pictures: people, animals, and objects. Ask your child to follow these instructions:

Time: 30–40 minutes

Materials
- 2 8½ × 11-inch sheets of heavy construction paper
- rounded-edge scissors

1. Fold the top left corner of a piece of paper until it reaches the right side of the page and makes a fold. It should look like a triangle with a rectangle below it.

 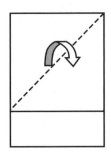 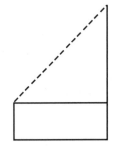

2. Cut off the rectangular piece at the bottom, which will leave you with a folded triangle. Open up the triangle to make a square. Cut the square in half at the fold. Now you have two triangles!

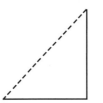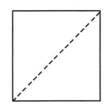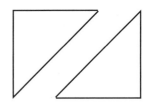

3. Take one triangle and fold it in half. Cut along the fold to make two smaller triangles.

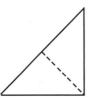

4. Take one of the smaller triangles and crease it down the middle. Open it up. Fold the corner of the triangle, matching the crease marks, until the tip reaches the long edge. Now, the tip of the larger triangle has a smaller triangle at the top. Cut it out.

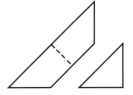

5. You now have a trapezoid with a fold in the middle. Cut on the fold.

6. Take one small trapezoid and fold it in half so that it looks like a triangle on top of a square. Open it up and cut on the fold, which will leave you with a small triangle and a small square.

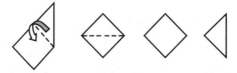

7. The other small trapezoid should be folded as shown and then cut.

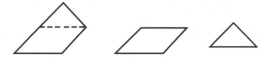

8. Now, you have all seven pieces of your tangram puzzle!

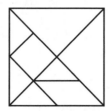

When you and your child are finished making the tangram, talk about the different shapes. How many triangles are there? How are they different? What four-sided shapes are there? Let your child play with the pieces and use his imagination to create all sort of things. There are some rules to playing with the tangram pieces. The classic rules are that you must use all seven tans, they must lay flat, they must touch, and none may overlap.

Variations: Check out www.knowledgeessentials.com to find more tangram puzzles.

🦻 Ask your child to tell you what each piece is and how many sides it has. Ask him to explain to you how to separate the pieces into groups according to shape.

👁 Ask your child to create a tangram pattern of his own for *you* to try and figure out. Let your child come up with his own pattern and trace the outline. Then see if you can figure out how to make it with the tangram pieces.

✋ Folding paper into shapes? Your kinesthetic child is going to eat this up like candy.

Mastery occurs when: your child can identify and manipulate the shapes used in the tangram puzzle.

You may want to help your child a little more if: he confuses the less common shapes. Review the shapes with your child and ask him to point out the shapes he sees every day. The more immersed and aware your child becomes, the easier the activity will be.

8 Dream House

TIME: 20–30 minutes

MATERIALS
- realty listing with pictures of the houses
- construction paper
- rounded-edge scissors
- nontoxic glue
- crayons and markers

Learning happens when: you and your child take a look at the types of houses in the realty listing. What kinds of shapes are used in building the houses? Ask your child to pick out all the different shapes she can see. Talk with your child about what kind of house she would build out of all those shapes. Give her different colored pieces of construction paper and a pair of scissors. Help her cut out various shapes. Ask her to glue the shapes onto a piece of construction paper to create her own dream house. She can use the crayons and markers to decorate the finished house.

Variations: Ask your child to use paper shapes to build a skate park, her school, or anything that interests her.

🦻 Talk with your child about the different shapes she is using. Why does that triangle make a great choice for a roof? How many things can you use a rectangle for? A door? A chimney? A window?

👁 Find examples of mosaics for your child to look at. Talk about the different shapes and colors and how they are combined to create a pattern or a design.

✋ Instead of using the realty listings, go for a walk or a drive around the neighborhood to look at houses.

Mastery occurs when: your child can identify all of the different shapes she used and can talk about characteristics of those shapes.

You may want to help your child a little more if: she is having trouble figuring out what the shapes are. Pick out one house to focus on and ask your child to highlight all the squares in one color. Then, using a different color, move on to another shape so that your child can differentiate between the shapes.

9 Shapes Collage

Learning happens when: you and your child draw shapes on the pieces of construction paper. Make triangles, squares, circles, parallelograms, hexagons, trapezoids, and rhombuses. (You can find these shapes at www.knowledgeessentials.com.) Print them, cut them out, trace them on a box top or other cardboard, and label them. Your child can now use the patterns you just made to help him draw the shapes until it becomes second nature. Create

TIME: 20 minutes

MATERIALS
- markers
- construction paper
- rounded-edge scissors
- nontoxic glue
- poster board
- pencil

different colors and sizes. Ask your child to glue these to the poster board as desired to create a geometric collage. After your child is finished, discuss what shapes he used and why.

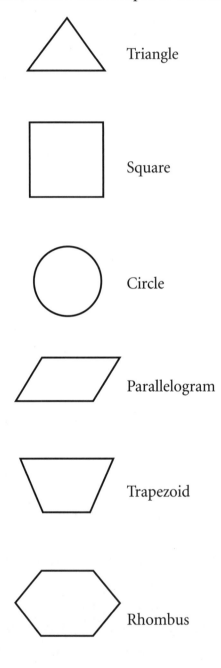

Triangle

Square

Circle

Parallelogram

Trapezoid

Rhombus

🦻 While you're working on this activity, talk with your child about the different aspects of shapes. How many sides does a rectangle have? A triangle? A circle? How many corners does each shape have? Try singing silly songs about shapes while you are making them. You can find the words to "Help Me Rhombus" at www.knowledgeessentials.com.

👁 Have your child use the shapes to make a sign or a scene. Does he have a sick friend? Make a get-well card with the shapes. Did your family just get back from a great vacation? Ask your child to re-create a favorite memory using the shapes.

✋ On a grander scale, try this activity outdoors using various sticks, rocks, or other natural shapes to create a collage on the grass.

Mastery occurs when: your child can draw and identify different shapes.

You may want to help your child a little more if: he has difficulty drawing the shapes. Let your child start by using stencils to make the shapes or trace other objects. Make sure he knows what shape it is by asking him while he traces.

Environmental Learning

Math is a great subject to practice every day. It's so easy to help your child practice the skills he will be using in school. Discuss shapes on your drive to school. Practice using money with a savings account or allowance. Measure a few feet out in the backyard for a garden. Check the temperature each morning to see what to wear. Math is easy to find and easy to practice every day with your potential Nobel Prize winner.

End of Second Grade Math Checklist

Students who are working at the standard level at the end of second grade:

____ Add and subtract two-and-three-digit numbers

____ Collect and compare seasonal temperatures using a thermometer

____ Use time to sequence events of the day

____ Recognize, identify, and create a circle, quadrilateral, rhombus, square, triangle, trapezoid, hexagon, and parallelogram

____ Compare and contrast the characteristics of shapes

____ Model and find the perimeter of simple shapes

____ Estimate and measure length, weight, and capacity using standard units of measurement

____ Use appropriate tools and terms to explore measurement

Second Grade Science

8

Second grade science teaches your child to plan and conduct simple investigations. This strengthens skills from reading, writing, and math—for example, making measurements using tools, such as rulers and clocks, to collect information, record observations, classify and sequence objects and events, and identify patterns. As your child learns science skills, he or she is identifying components of the natural world, including the water cycle and the use of resources. Your child will observe melting and evaporation, weathering, and the pushing and pulling of objects as the result of change. The solar system and objects in it are studied. Additionally, second graders compare the lifelong needs of plants and animals (including humans), understand how living organisms depend on their environments, and identify the functions of the parts of plants and animals.

Beginning of Second Grade Science Checklist

Students who are working at the standard level at the beginning of second grade:

____ Identify and describe bodies of water and marine life

____ Can make observations and recognize similarities and differences

____ Categorize living and nonliving things and systems

____ Understand that there are a variety of earth materials

____ Describe life stages, particularly of butterflies or tadpoles

---

The Human Body

Your child probably has a good start on this concept from activities in first grade and gym class, and from general life experience. In second grade your child will refine these skills by:

- Learning about the parts of the human body and their functions
- Learning about the things that keep a person healthy, such as exercise and healthy food choices

Your child will be studying the skeletal system and learning about calcium for healthy bones. Second graders also study the major organs and what they do, especially the heart. The five senses are further examined in second grade.

The following table describes some important concepts related to the human body, where children can run into problems, and what you can to do to help them along.

Human Body Concepts	Having Problems?	Quick Tips
Discerns each of the five senses.	Mixes up the names of the five senses.	Use an anagram, flash cards, or any tool that aids your child's memory. At this age, your child knows which sense does what—it is simply a memory issue to get the names down.
Knows what healthy choices are and makes them.	Does not understand why it is important to make healthy choices and/or doesn't make them.	Model healthy living as much as you possibly can around your child and talk about why you are doing it. Point out the effects of not making healthy choices when possible and praise your child when he or she makes a healthy choice, such as choosing juice or water over soda, choosing fruit as a snack, or remembering to put on sunscreen.

The Human Body Activities

1 Sense-ible Walk

Learning happens when: you and your child take a walk on a local trail or to a nearby park. Try the following with your child:

TIME: 30 minutes

- While walking, pick up different things along the way without your child noticing. Some good items include leaves, a feather, a flower, and a twig. Ask your child to stop and close his eyes. Ask him to guess what the item is by using his sense of touch.

- While you and your child are stopped, have him listen to the sounds. Are birds chirping? Was that a child laughing? Is that a squeaky swing?

- Ask your child to keep his eyes closed and breathe deeply. Ask him to describe what smells are in the air.

- Let your child open his eyes and look around. Ask him to look down at the ground closely and describe what he sees. Then, have him look up at the sky (just not at the sun) and do the same.

Mastery occurs when: your child can use a variety of senses to identify things around him.

Variations: Try a city or town walk instead of a nature walk.

- Talk with your child about which of the five senses he might use the most. It's a difficult question—it's surprising how often you use your senses. Ask your child to tell you when he notices the use of a certain sense that he is generally unaware of.

👁 Make a chart with your child with the five senses as the column headings. Ask your child to fill in different things that a person does with each sense.

✌ Try a trust walk (this is best in a familiar area). Blindfold your child and lead him around. Ask him what he hears, smells, and feels. Then, trade spots to let your child use his sense of sight to lead you.

You may want to help your child a little more if: he is having difficulty identifying things. You may want to isolate this activity by using one sense at a time in a more secluded area. Start with sight because that is generally the most used sense and continue from there.

2 | Tasty . . . Right?

TIME: 20 minutes

MATERIALS
blindfold
nose plug
knife
cutting board
various fruits and
vegetables, such as
apples or carrots
paper
pencils

Learning happens when: you and your child talk about the sense of taste. What helps you taste? The obvious answers are the mouth and the tongue, but ask your child about her sense of smell. Does your sense of smell help you taste? This activity will test that question.

Cover your child's eyes with the blindfold. Ask your child to place the nose plug on her nose (make sure to remind your child to breathe though the mouth) to stop her sense of smell. Cut up different types of fruits and vegetables and feed them to your child one at a time. After each piece, ask your child to try and identify what she is eating and write it down. When you're finished with all of the tasting, let your child take off the blindfold and nose plug and look at the results. They can be surprising!

Variations: You can do this with food your child won't usually try. Your child may be surprised to find out that she likes mango . . . or string beans.

🦻 Talk with your child about how senses work together. How does your sense of sight help your sense of touch? (An example is putting your hand down on a stove, unable to see that it's not a counter.) How does your sense of hearing help your sense of sight? (An example is hearing a car horn and turning to see the car coming toward you.) How does your sense of smell help your sense of taste in the nose plug and blindfold activity?

👁 After the activity, give your child a few sheets of paper. Ask her to draw the foods that she liked the taste of the most. Then, ask your child to write a few sentences describing the taste and texture.

✋ Try this activity again, but let your child touch the entire fruit or vegetable before you cut it. Did the sense of touch make it easier to figure out what she was eating when she tasted it?

Mastery occurs when: your child understands how the sense of smell affects the sense of taste.

You may want to help your child a little more if: she is unwilling to try the different foods. Let your child go with you to the grocery store and pick out fruits and vegetables that interest her.

3 | Calisthenics

Learning happens when: you and your child go to a park that has a jungle gym, a slide, swings, and balance beams. Tell your child that you're going to test his cardiovascular health. Talk with your child about the importance of exercise for being healthy. Exercise is most effective when the heart rate is increased. Show your child how to find his heart rate by putting the index and middle fingers

TIME: 30 minutes

MATERIALS
- jump rope
- watch with a second hand
- small notepad
- pencils

on the inside of the wrist right under the thumb. Have your child count the number of heartbeats felt in ten seconds. Ask him to add the result to itself six times (that is, multiply it by 6). That is your child's resting heart rate.

Make up a short obstacle course for your child, such as:

Ten jumping jacks

Ten swings on the monkey bars

Ten rotations with the jumping jacks (turn in a circle while doing a jumping jack)

Ten seconds on the swings

Ten times down the slide

Ten seconds of running in place

Make sure your child counts the repetitions aloud. Then, have him recheck his heart rate. Talk with your child about why the heart rate went up. Talk about other ways to exercise to keep his body healthy. You and your child can keep an exercise journal to track progress.

Variations: Find an organization that does walkathons and sign up with your child. Not only is it a great way to get exercise and up your heart rate, you can help a worthy cause at the same time.

- Talk with your child about activities that are good for cardiovascular health. Brainstorm some ways to keep the family physically fit.

- Ask your child to draw a picture of an activity that is good for the body. Help him write a few sentences underneath the picture to describe the activity and why it is beneficial.

- Invent a family triathlon! It doesn't matter what three things you decide on, because a triathlon is just an event with three separate parts. Go traditional with swimming, biking, and jogging, or get creative and pick your own activities.

Mastery occurs when: your child can understand the significance of exercise to a healthy body.

You may want to help your child a little more if: he has a disability or is otherwise unable to perform these activities. Ask your child to do less intensive exercises, such as touching his toes or making arm circles. Any amount of physical exertion should raise your child's heart rate.

4 Body Map

Learning happens when: you and your child talk about some of the important organs of the body and what they do. Some major organs to discuss are the heart, the lungs, the brain, the stomach, the intestines, the liver, the kidneys, and the bladder. (Feel free to discuss other parts with your child as well, since this is just an overview of the basics.)

Take the large piece of paper and lay it flat on the ground. Ask your child to lie down and trace around her. Then ask your child where on the body each organ is found. After she answers, ask your child to double-check using the encyclopedia or books. When your child has confirmed where the organ is located, let her draw it on the outline. Continue until your child has created her own organ map.

Variations: You can use the same outline to map out the circulatory system, the muscles, or the skeletal structure. Check in an encyclopedia or book on the human body to make sure that everything is correct.

TIME: 30–45 minutes

MATERIALS
- large sheet of butcher paper
- pencils
- encyclopedia and books on the human body
- crayons and markers

◗ Look at the body map with your child and talk about what each organ does in the body. How are the organs connected? What do they do to help keep you going?

◉ If you'd like to make this a more singular activity, ask your child to take a sheet of paper and choose one part of the body to focus on. Have your child draw a picture of what she chose and then write three facts about it.

✋ Ask your child to stand up. Say the name of an organ aloud and ask your child to point to where it is in her body (check with a reference book if you're not sure).

Mastery occurs when: your child can identify the major organs of the body, what they do, and where they are.

You may want to help your child a little more if: she is having trouble remembering where each organ is located in the body. Start from the top—with the brain, then the lungs, then the heart, and so on. This will help reinforce where each organ is in the body.

5 Healthy Snacks

TIME: 20 minutes

MATERIALS
▪ food magazines
▪ rounded-edge scissors
▪ paper
▪ pencils
▪ nontoxic glue

Learning happens when: you ask your child what he thinks is a good snack. Cookies, candy, and the occasional fruit will probably come up. Ask your child what the difference is between his answers and healthy snacks.

Give your child the magazines to look through and ask him to cut out pictures of healthy food and unhealthy food. Fold the paper in half and label one column "Healthy Foods" and the other "Unhealthy Foods." Help your child to glue the pictures of the healthy foods and the unhealthy foods in the appropriate column. Hang the finished project on the refrigerator to help remind *all* family members what options there are for healthy eating!

When your child comes home from school, ask him to help you choose between two snacks. One should be a healthy treat, the other one a little less healthy. Talk with your child about which one is a better snack option and why. Try this a few days out of the week with your child to help him better identify with the healthy snack.

Go on a hunt through your kitchen cabinets. Let your child help you to weed out the unhealthy foods by reading the nutrition labels on the side. Point out the daily values column and how vitamins and calories can add up!

After your child has made his collage of healthy foods, go to the grocery store and ask him to help you pick out some healthy foods for lunches and snacks.

Mastery occurs when: your child can identify healthy food options.

You may want to help your child a little more if: he has trouble picking out the healthy foods. Wander around the produce section and other aisles of your local supermarket. Point out the healthy foods to your child and let him help you choose a few to bring home.

The Solar System

Space . . . the final frontier. Well maybe not, but it can seem like that, especially to your second grader. What's out there anyway? What *are* stars? Why don't they all look the same? Where are these other planets? What's the moon made out of? There are a lot of questions about space with a lot of interesting answers.

Your child will be learning about the nine planets, the sun, the moon, and the constellations.

The following table describes some important concepts related to the solar system, where children can run into problems, and what you can do to help them along.

Solar System Concepts	Having Problems?	Quick Tips
Names the planets in our solar system.	Is unable to name the planets in our solar system.	Use a mnemonic device to help your child remember. Try **M**y **V**ery **E**asy **M**ethod **J**ust **S**tarted **U** **N**aming **P**lanets (beginning with the planet closest to the sun: Mercury, Venus, Earth, Mars, Jupiter, Saturn, Uranus, Neptune, and Pluto).
Understands that many stars are grouped together visually, and those groups are called constellations.	Is unable to understand that groups of stars are called constellations.	Start with just one constellation that is easy to see by locating the Big Dipper in the night sky. It is easy to see and to understand why it is called the Big Dipper.

The Solar System Activities

1 Closer Constellations

TIME: 30 minutes

MATERIALS
- book about constellations
- black paper cut into 3-inch squares
- pencils
- flashlight

Learning happens when: you and your child take a look at the night sky on a clear evening. What can you see? How many stars can you count? Can you see any patterns in them? Take a look at the book of constellations and see if your child can locate any in the night sky. Remember, some constellations are only visible at certain times of the year.

After finding the constellations in the sky, make some inside. Give your child the paper, a pencil, and the flashlight. Using the book as a guide, let your child punch small holes into the paper, using the point of the pencil, in the formation of a constellation.

Turn off the lights and ask your child to turn on the flashlight and put the paper over the top of the light. Turn the flashlight toward the ceiling. Now, no matter what time of the year it is, your child can have an indoor night sky full of constellations.

Variations: Ask your child to create his own constellation. Then have your child name it and write a story to explain it.

- Talk with your child about the stories that surround some of the constellations. Ask your child to tell you about the story that could go along with his constellation.

- Go outside during different months to observe the changes in the constellations. Discuss with your child why certain constellations are only visible at a certain time of the year.

- Explore a science museum or planetarium with your child. A planetarium can show you all the different constellations throughout the year in about a half hour!

Mastery occurs when: your child can identify constellations in the sky.

You may want to help your child a little more if: he has difficulty finding the constellations. It may be easier for your child to play connect the dots first by plotting out the pattern on a sheet of paper and drawing a line between them. He can use that pattern to compare to the ones in the night sky.

2 Planetary Postcards

Learning happens when: you and your child read *Postcards from Pluto*. Discuss the book. Ask your child which planet she liked the most. What would you write on a postcard if you visited that

Time: 30 minutes

MATERIALS
- *Postcards from Pluto* by Loreen Leedy
- crayons
- index cards
- pencils
- reference materials on the planets

planet? Ask your child to draw a picture of her favorite planet on the unlined side of an index card. On the other side, let your child write a postcard to someone (you may want to help steer this to a grandparent). Ask your child to write a few facts about the planet on the postcard, using the reference materials if needed. Include a short note to the person receiving the postcard, then mail it!

Variations: Ask your child to pretend she is exploring one of the nine planets. You are her commander back on Earth and your child needs to report back to you about what the planet is like. Have your child write a short report to you back on Earth.

- Review what your child has learned in the book by discussing the planets with her. What interesting facts about each planet did your child learn? Which planet was her favorite? Can your child describe that planet to you?

- Ask your child to write a poem or a short story about how she imagines it would be to live on one of the planets.

- Give your child various art materials, such as Styrofoam, paint, paper, and glue, and help her to create a planet. Make sure to add features such as craters or mountains to the planet as well.

Mastery occurs when: your child can research and relay information about the planets.

You may want to help your child a little more if: she has difficulty remembering the planets. Use a mnemonic device to help your child remember. Try **M**y **V**ery **E**asy **M**ethod **J**ust **S**tarted **U** **N**aming **P**lanets (beginning with the planet closest to the sun: Mercury, Venus, Earth, Mars, Jupiter, Saturn, Uranus, Neptune, and Pluto). Let your child make up a mnemonic device of her own.

3 | Travel Agent

TIME: 30 minutes

MATERIALS
- travel brochures for trips to multiple places
- pencils
- paper
- reference materials on the planets
- crayons and markers

Learning happens when: you and your child look over the travel brochures. What kind of information do they have in them? What do they explain? What do they try to do? Now ask your child to think about planning a trip to the nine planets. Ask him to make a list of the nine planets and underneath each planet to write down three interesting facts. Using that information, ask your child to make a travel brochure for a trip from planet to planet.

- Pretend that you and your child are on a tour of the planets and let your child be the tour guide. Take a drive or a walk and let your child pretend that you're in space going past the planets. Make sure to ask questions about each planet so that your child can tell you all the interesting facts he knows!

- Go to a planetarium or a science museum with your child to learn more about the planets. Planetariums generally show stars, but they do point out where and when you can see certain planets in the night sky.

- Using foam balls of various sizes from a craft store, let your child write the name of a planet and some facts about it on each ball with a marker.

Mastery occurs when: your child can recall and use information about the nine planets in our solar system.

You may want to help your child a little more if: he is having trouble recalling facts about each planet. Start with one planet. Ask your child to make a brochure for that planet. Then, once you're child is comfortable, move on to another.

4 Moonshine

TIME: 10 minutes

MATERIALS
- room with blinds
- black paper
- tape
- flashlight

Learning happens when: you and your child discuss how the moon shines. Why can't we usually see the moon in the daytime? Where does it go? Close the blinds and tape the black paper to the wall. Give your child the flashlight and ask her to stand across the room, opposite the construction paper. Turn off any lights and ask your child to shine the light on the paper. Keeping the flashlight on, turn on the lights and open the blinds. What happened to the light on the paper? The light from the sun is so bright that you can't see the light from the flashlight anymore. The sun does the same thing to the moonlight during the day. Ask your child if she now understands why the moon can't usually be seen during the day.

- Ask your child to describe the properties of the moon and why sometimes it can be seen and sometimes it can't be seen.

- Kids love anything that glows in the dark. Get stickers, slimy goo, or whatever glows. It's not quite the same principle, but it gets the point across. When the light is on, the glowing isn't visible. But turn the light out, and poof! It's glowing!

- Try this activity with your child at dusk. Use a flashlight and every few minutes, as the sun is setting, ask your child to walk outside and check to see if the light from the flashlight can be seen. How long did it take to see the light?

Mastery occurs when: your child can understand that the sun and the moon both rise and set, but there is a part of each day when you can see both. During most of the day the sun's light is too strong for the reflected light of the moon to be seen, but when the sun is setting or rising, the light isn't as strong, so you can see the sun and the moon.

You may want to help your child a little more if: she has trouble understanding that the sun can cause the moon to disappear in the daytime. Try to explain to your child that the sun's light is so bright during the day that it completely outshines the moon. At night, the moon reflects the sun's light so that you can see it.

5 Sunny S'mores

Learning happens when: you talk with your child about how hot the sun is. Ask your child to guess how hot the sun is. The part of the sun we can see is 11,000 degrees Fahrenheit. The core of the sun is 27 million degrees Fahrenheit! So what can you do with all that heat? Make s'mores! This activity will show the power of the sun. (This activity must be done on a sunny day.)

TIME: 1–2 hours

MATERIALS
- ruler
- pencils
- pizza box
- rounded-edge scissors
- aluminum foil
- nontoxic glue
- sheet of clear, heavy plastic
- tape
- black construction paper
- graham crackers
- marshmallows
- chocolate bars
- oven thermometer
- straw or stick

1. Use the ruler to draw a one-inch border around the top of the pizza box. Cut along three of the sides, leaving the back of the box uncut. Fold back the flap you've made.

2. Ask your child to cut a piece of foil to fit on the inside of the flap and glue it into place.

3. Your child should measure a piece of plastic to fit over the opening in the top of the pizza box. The plastic needs to be larger than the hole so that it can be taped to the underside of the flap. Make sure that your child tapes the plastic down tight, so that it's a complete seal.

4. Ask your child to cut another piece of foil to line the bottom of the pizza box and glue it down.

5. Have your child cover the foil with a piece of black construction paper and tape it.

6. Ask your child to put together s'mores and place them on the black construction paper in the pizza box.

7. Give your child the oven thermometer to put into the box to see just how warm the sun can make the box.

8. Take the box outside. Close the plastic top and prop open the flap of the box with the straw or stick so that the foil is aimed toward the sun. Keep an eye on the solar oven, and in a little while, you'll have perfectly melted s'mores.

👂 Talk with your child about how much heat is needed to cook things. Take a look at a cookbook or a chart of recommended cooking temperatures for foods. Discuss how those temperatures compare to the temperature of the solar oven.

👁 Depending on how brightly the sun is shining, you can cook a variety of things. Try mini pizzas, cookies, even clay! Play with the solar oven on different days and compare the temperatures inside.

✋ This activity was practically *made* for kinesthetic learners—do this activity as suggested.

Mastery occurs when: your child can comprehend the amount of heat the sun can give off.

You may want to help your child a little more if: he is having trouble understanding how the sun's powerful rays translate into heat. When you were a child, on a really sunny, warm day, did you ever fry an egg on the sidewalk? Try it with your child, especially if you've got a spot of asphalt to do it on. While you're frying, discuss how the sun is heating up the ground, making it warm enough to cook the egg. The black pavement of the street or driveway absorbs more heat than the lighter colored concrete of the sidewalk and causes the egg to fry faster.

The Earth, the Seasons, and the Weather

I'll bet that when your child is getting dressed in the morning, he or she asks you, "What's it supposed to be like today?" Children learn in kindergarten and first grade that if they wear the wrong clothes they can end up too hot or too cold, and worse yet, if they don't bring a coat and it is cold they may not be able to go outside for recess. Temperature, weather, and the changing seasons are all part of living on Earth and a part of second grade science.

Your child will be learning how Earth's tilt creates the seasons. He or she will also be discovering what makes the changes in our weather. The following table describes some important concepts related to seasons and weather, where children can run into problems, and what you can do to help them along.

Seasons and Weather Concepts	Having Problems?	Quick Tips
Understands that there are different types of clouds.	Is unable to identify different types of clouds.	Ask your child to draw a cloud chart or make up a cloud chant. Talk about what type of clouds you see outside on a regular basis.
Identifies weather events that could be unsafe.	Has difficulty relating the personal implications of weather events.	Talk about weather safety every time the unsafe weather event occurs. Talk about why it is unsafe to do certain things while the weather is that way and how to be safe during those times.

Earth, Seasons, and Weather Activities

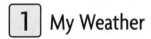 My Weather

Learning happens when: you and your child take a look at the local five-day forecast online or on the television. How can the weather be predicted that far in advance? Is it always right? Look up the

TIME: 20 minutes

MATERIALS
▪ weather Web site or
television channel
▪ pencils
▪ paper
▪ crayons or markers

weather forecast from the week before and have your child compare it to the actual weather from the past week. How accurate was it? Show your child the Doppler radar of the country. Point out how weather in the middle part of the country can affect the weather where you live.

Ask your child to look at the Doppler and try to predict the weather for the next few days. Have him use pictures to illustrate his predictions and then post them somewhere your child can see them and compare. When the designated days are up, talk with your child about how accurate he was. Was it easy to predict the weather correctly? Why or why not?

- Talk with your child about the weather. How fast can the weather change? Does it change every day? What signs are there that the weather might change soon?

- Watch the local weather channel with your child in the morning to see what the weather will be like that day. If you don't have a local weather channel you can use the newspaper or the Internet.

- Play weather forecaster. Let your child make a map of the country and add any weather patterns that might be approaching. Then let your child be your weatherman.

Mastery occurs when: your child can use the Doppler to predict weather and understand how meteorologists attempt to predict the weather.

You may want to help your child a little more if: he cannot use the Doppler to predict future weather patterns. Actually seeing the Doppler moving is a good start. There are many Web sites that offer free weather radar monitoring. Ask your child to watch the radar and see if he can determine what types of weather different areas are experiencing.

2 What's in a Cloud?

Learning happens when: you and your child talk about clouds. Go outside on a partly cloudy day and look at the sky. What is a cloud made of? Clouds are a big collection of water droplets or ice crystals that are pushed by air currents. Ask your child what gray clouds mean. What about white fluffy clouds? Wispy clouds?

TIME: 20–30 minutes

MATERIALS
- blue paper
- cotton balls
- nontoxic glue
- markers

Clouds are indicators for weather. The three basic types of clouds are cirrus, cumulus, and stratus. Cirrus clouds are the wispy-looking clouds high up in the sky. Cumulus clouds are the big, white, fluffy clouds you can see on a sunny day. Stratus clouds look like a grey blanket in the sky. On some days more than one type of cloud will be visible.

Ask your child to illustrate what the sky looks like by gluing the cotton balls to the paper. Then have her label the clouds according to type.

- While you're out and about during the day, ask your child to point out what kinds of clouds are in the sky and to describe what they look like to you.

- Ask your child to monitor the sky for a week at the same time of day. Let her illustrate the clouds for each day of the week. If there is a thunderstorm, your child can label the clouds as cumulonimbus, which is a thunderhead. If it is raining or snowing, your child can name the clouds as nimbostratus. Any variation of the word "nimbus" with a cloud name refers to precipitation.

- Take a walk with your child to a nearby park, or maybe just as far as your backyard—anywhere there's an unobstructed view of the sky and a comfortable place to lie down. Lying on your backs, take a look at the clouds in the sky. What kinds are there? How do you know? Are there any funny shapes?

Mastery occurs when: your child can identify the three major types of clouds and what they mean.

You may want to help your child a little more if: she is confusing the types of clouds. The best way to get used to the types of clouds is to watch for them. While you're driving in the car, walking in the park, or just hanging out in the backyard, ask what's going on with the clouds. Practice helps!

3 | Weather Writing

TIME: 15–20 minutes

MATERIALS
- book of nature poems
- pictures of different types of weather
- paper
- pencils

Learning happens when: you and your child read some of the nature poems together. Ask him to read at least one aloud. Discuss the poems you read and what they have in common. Are some about rain or snow? Was it warm or cold?

Ask your child to think of a particular weather-related event that he remembers. Was this a good memory, like a rainbow after a rainstorm? Or was it scary, like a tornado or a hurricane? What happened? How did it turn out? How did he feel after it was over?

- 👂 After discussing his weather-related incident, ask your child to write a poem about it and then read it aloud.

- 👁 Ask your child to make an illustration for one of the poems that he enjoyed. If your child is really creative, ask him to write a nature poem and draw a picture to accompany it.

- ✋ Have your child write a short skit about a weather-related event and then help act it out. Maybe your child will want to change how he dealt with the event.

Mastery occurs when: your child can discuss the poems he read about and describe his own weather experience.

You may want to help your child a little more if: he is having trouble thinking of a weather-related event. Take a walk or look outside. It's as easy as watching the clouds morph, or the leaves change, or the snow fall. It doesn't have to be a catastrophic event; it could be the clean smell after a rain shower, or the bright sunshine reflecting off the lake.

4 | Lightning Safety

Learning happens when: you and your child talk about lightning. What is lightning? It's a big charge of electricity from the atmosphere. Generally, lightning is associated with a thunderstorm, but there's also dry lightning and heat lightning that don't require any rain at all.

TIME: 30 minutes

MATERIALS

paper
pencils

Ask your child if she knows what to do when thunder starts. Have your child fold the paper in half and label one column "Indoors" and the other "Outdoors." What should you do if you are outside and you hear thunder or see lightning? Help your child think of some safety rules and write them in the appropriate column. Some basic outdoor safety rules include avoiding water and metal, and not taking shelter under trees. Then ask your child to think about lightning safety indoors. Again, there are some basics to remember, such as not talking on the phone, staying away from doors and windows, and avoiding water (this is probably the only time your child can get away with not taking a bath). There are more safety rules that you can find online. Post the finished chart in a visible area of your house, as a reminder to everyone in the family.

Variations: If you live in an area where other natural disasters are an issue, such as tornadoes, hurricanes, or earthquakes, make plans for these events. Don't forget that topics like natural disasters are sometimes overwhelming and can make your child anxious. Having a plan in case one should happen is a good way to help alleviate any anxiety or fears your child has.

- 👂 Make sure to talk with your child regularly about the safety rules for lightning. The more you talk about it, the easier it will be for your child to remember if the need ever arises.

- 👁 Ask your child to add illustrations to the list of safety rules and post them somewhere in the house. The visual representations will not only help your visual learner remember them, it could also help any younger children you may have who can't read.

- ✍ Practice the plans with your child and the rest of the family by acting them out.

Mastery occurs when: your child understands the power of lightning and how to avoid dangerous situations.

You may want to help your child a little more if: she has difficulty remembering the safety rules for lightning. Practice with your child. On a nice day, go outside and practice what your child should do when she hears thunder or sees lightning. When you're indoors, ask your child randomly about what to do if she hears thunder or sees lightning. The repetition will help your child remember what to do.

5 | Seasons

Learning happens when: you talk with your child about how the globe is situated. Why do you think it matters that Earth is tilted? Ask your child to tell you about the seasons. Most probably, your child will tell you about the weather associated with the changing seasons as opposed to what causes the seasonal change. Talk with your child about how Earth orbits the sun. Ask your child to be Earth. Have him hold the globe out in front with one hand at the top and the other at the bottom so that he can simulate Earth's orbit. You pretend you're the sun. Turn on the flashlight. Ask your child to walk around you and the light, slowly turning the globe (make sure he keeps Earth on its axis). As your child orbits you, have him stop every few seconds to see which part of Earth is tilted toward the light. Ask your child which part of Earth is hotter and which is colder. Then, discuss how this causes the changes in the seasons.

TIME: 20 minutes

MATERIALS

globe that is tilted on its axis

flashlight

- Ask your child to teach *you* about the tilt and orbit of Earth. Go through the activity once or twice with your child, then switch roles and *you* be the student. See if your child can explain to you what's going on.

- Try videotaping this activity as you do it with your child. After you and your child have completed the activity, sit down together and watch the video. Turn down the volume and ask your child to tell you what's going on and what it means in terms of the seasons.

- This activity is already a great one for your kinesthetic learner! Try it as is.

Mastery occurs: when your child can understand how Earth's axis and orbit cause the seasons.

You may want to help your child a little more if: he has trouble understanding the concept of the seasonal changes caused by the tilt in Earth's axis. Try the activity again and talk with your child about the angle of the sun's rays. Ask your child questions such as, "Is a straight ray of light hotter than one that isn't straight?"

Environmental Learning

Whether you know it, you talk about science every day. What's the weather going to be tomorrow? Is it going to be cold enough to snow? What do you wear in the summer? It's an everyday topic that you and your child can expand on.

The human body is another topic you probably talk about daily, especially if you have a very active child. Running, swimming, and soccer all use the body's systems. Does the child fall down? Bumps, bruises, and scrapes can be explained as part of the body's healing mechanism. A great way to get science into your child's day is having your child help you pick out healthy snacks and make nourishing meals.

Although space and the solar system don't seem like subjects that come up often, it's not uncommon to remark about the moon or the stars in the evening. You and your child may even look for shooting stars!

End of Second Grade Science Checklist

Students who are working at the standard level at the end of second grade:

____ Identify various constellations

____ Can associate Earth's axis and orbit with seasonal changes

____ Identify the nine planets

____ Understand the importance of exercise and good diet for a healthy body

____ Recognize different types of clouds and the weather they predict

____ Can explain the importance of the senses

Second Grade
Social Studies

9

Social studies in second grade is a lot like social studies in first grade, when children learn about where they are in the world and that the world has rules they need to follow. They have learned that they live in a country called the United States of America and that our country has national symbols, songs, and holidays. So where do they go from here? They move on to more of the basics of the world they live in and how to relate to it.

This year your child starts learning about geography and map skills, starting with the geographic characteristics of their neighborhood. Neighborhood concepts expand from geography and map skills to the economic roles their neighbors play, the goods and services they produce and purchase, and the neighborhood services governments provide. Second graders will also be learning about the rules that govern us: who makes them, what they mean, and how to follow them.

> ### Beginning of Second Grade Social Studies Checklist
>
> Students working on the standard level at the beginning of second grade:
>
> ____ Know the name of their country
>
> ____ Know the name of their state
>
> ____ Know and follow school and community rules
>
> ____ Understand that there are places, usually called landmarks, that have special meaning to people
>
> ____ Name and understand meaning of major U.S. holidays

Communities

At this point your little one knows what a community is. He or she can tell you about many types—including communities of people and communities of animals. Your child can probably pick out community workers and helpers that he or she sees every day, such as police officers or bank tellers. If you and your child have ever visited another community, your child can probably compare and contrast the features of your community and the one you visited. In second grade, your child will continue to focus on what a community is and what it needs to function properly.

The following table describes some important concepts related to communities, where children can run into problems, and what you can do to help them along.

Communities Concepts	Having Problems?	Quick Tips
Understands that groups of people live in many different ways.	Thinks that all groups of people live in a community just like the one that he or she lives in.	Talk about the setting of any book you are reading with your child and ask what type of community is featured in the book. Talk about how communities you visit are alike and different from your own.

Communities Activities

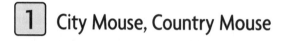 **City Mouse, Country Mouse**

Learning happens when: you and your child read the story of the city mouse and the country mouse together. Ask your child to write "The City" on the left side of the large sheet of paper and

"The Country" on the right side. Give your child the index cards and ask him to write down details about the city community. Where did the mouse live? What did he eat? What did he do for fun? Ask your child to write down all the things he remembers about the country community. How was the community the country mouse lived in different? Mix up the cards, then ask your child to draw one at a time. He should then tape the card on the side of the paper where it belongs. Look at the chart you and your child have made and talk about how each column relates or doesn't relate to the community you live in.

Variations: Try the same activity with different geographical areas, such as the ocean, mountains, or the forest.

TIME: 20–30 minutes

MATERIALS

- story of the city mouse and the country mouse (from a book or on the Internet)
- pencils
- large sheet of paper
- index cards
- tape

- Ask your child to draw what he liked about the country mouse's community and then that of the city mouse. Which would he rather live in? Why?

- There is a great Tom and Jerry cartoon that tells the story of the two mice really well. You may want to find this and watch it with your child.

- If you live in the country, take a trip into the city. If you live in the city, take a trip out to the country. Talk with your child about the differences between where you are visiting and where you live.

Mastery occurs when: your child can pick out the differences in the communities.

You may want to help your child a little more if: he has difficulty pointing out the differences in the two communities. Instead of waiting until the end of the story to pick out the details, let your child write out the details as you read the story together.

2 | Come See Where I Live!

TIME: 30 minutes

MATERIALS
brochures or posters
that show various
communities and their
special characteristics
(a school, a city, a vacation destination)
pencils
construction paper
rounded-edge scissors
nontoxic glue
crayons

Learning happens when: you and your child look over the brochures about various communities. What pictures do the brochures show? What information do they include? Why do you think they might want to tell you about the great park instead of the shopping mall? After talking about the brochures, ask your child to make a list of important facts about where you live. Are there any interesting sites? What about things to do? When the list is finished, help your child to use the list to create her own brochure of your community.

Ask your child to do a mini presentation for you using her brochure as a visual. You may want to ask your child for a more detailed description of major attractions in your area.

Go out into the town and help your child take photos of important and interesting points in your town. Add them to the brochure to help illustrate it.

Travel somewhere outside of your town. Try going to an old colonial village or a museum exhibit about a time in the past. Ask your child to create a brochure about the community.

Mastery occurs when: your child can identify key points about her community and convey them in another format.

You may want to help your child a little more if: she cannot pick out important aspects of the community. Take a drive through your town. Ask your child to tell you about the sights and then use that information to make the brochure later.

3 | Map of the Community

Learning happens when: you and your child think about your community. Is it a large or a small community? What kinds of people make up the community? What kinds of jobs do they do? Where are they in the community? On a pleasant day, take a walk with your child around your town (if you live in a large city, feel free to drive or take a bus or train). Walk to the police station, the fire station, the school, and other places of importance in the community.

When you get home, help your child create a community map. Make the map as accurate as possible. Put it up somewhere in the house, preferably with the emergency numbers for your area.

TIME: 30–40 minutes

MATERIALS
construction paper
markers
pencils
ruler
crayons

- Ask your child to tell you how to get to different places in your community, such as the police station or his school. Your child may not be able to give you specific directions, but landmarks are a perfectly good way to navigate through town!

- Take a look at an official town map. See if your child can locate your house or his school. Maps with keys are a good starting point for this.

- Tour your community and stop in at important places such as the hospital or the police station. Let your child see what it's like inside. He might even be able to get a tour!

Mastery occurs when: your child can identify the important parts of a community and where they are in relation to his house.

You may want to help your child a little more if: he doesn't see how his home is part of the community. Get a real map of the town and look at it with your child. Mark out your street and the important community centers. Use that to help your child draw a map.

4 What's Going on Here?

TIME: 10–15 minutes

MATERIALS
▢ local daily newspaper

Peruse the paper before you show it to your child to check for unsuitable articles.

Learning happens when: you and your child take a look at the daily newspaper together. Most local papers come with a community section. Check out the current events for your area. This is a great thing to start doing daily. Not only does it keep you and your child up on current events, it promotes reading.

Variations: Ask your child to write a family community newsletter. She can write about what's been going on, upcoming events, and interesting facts about family members.

🦻 The local radio station is another option for finding out about what's going on in the community. Thursdays and Fridays are excellent times to find out what activities are going on in your area over the weekend.

👁 This activity is already a great one for your visual learner. Make it a daily habit.

✌ Your child can find all sorts of family events to go to in the newspaper. Pick one and go!

Mastery occurs when: your child can read the newspaper for current events and information about your community.

You may want to help your child a little more if: she finds the newspaper a little too much to read. Pick out an article that might be of interest to your child. Choose three a week instead of every day.

5 | In the Past

TIME: 20 minutes

MATERIALS
local historical area

Learning happens when: you and your child look up a nearby historical area. It could be a colonial or a Native American village, anything that your child finds interesting. Explore it with your child. Be a tour guide; talk about the differences between how people lived in the past and how we live today. If there isn't much information associated with the area, or if your child has questions you don't have answers for, go to the library and look up information about that time. Local libraries are a great place to find information about where you live. Let your child check out a book about children from that time. There are some great series, such as Laura Ingalls Wilder's *Little House on the Prairie* or the American Girls series.

Variations: If you can't find a nearby place to visit, go to the library with your child and look up books about a specific time. Ask your child to pick out the differences and similarities in the communities, past and present.

- Go on a historical tour, either somewhere in your town or to a museum of history. Let your child ask the guide questions.

- Go to a historical museum or other place that has historical artifacts. Look at all of the different items and talk with your child about how and why they are significant.

- Create history with your child. Make a time capsule or purchase a kit. Talk with your child about how things become historical. What things are important to your family at this point in time? Maybe your child is a sports fan; brainstorm things that could go into a time capsule to reflect that interest. Ask your child to write a note so that if one day someone digs up the capsule, he or she will know when it was buried and who made it.

Mastery occurs when: your child can notice details about and appreciate communities of the past.

You may want to help your child a little more if: he doesn't seem to get the connection of communities in the past to the present. Focus your discussions on the similarities and differences for a specific topic, such as schooling or games.

Government

Who is the boss of you? Who makes the rules in your house? What about your town? Your county? Your state? I'm sure by now your child knows who makes the rules in *your* house (although you might be surprised who it is!), but figuring out who's in charge outside the house is what your child is going to learn about at school.

The following table describes some important concepts related to government, where children can run into problems, and what you can do to help them along.

Government Concepts	Having Problems?	Quick Tips
Knows how rules that we live by as a society are made.	Has difficulty remembering how rules that we live by as a society are made.	There are lots of opportunities to talk about how and why laws are made and then how they are enforced on a regular basis, particularly traffic rules. Talk about traffic rules when driving with your child.
Knows that there are rules at home and at school and tries to observe them.	Breaks rules at home and at school on a regular basis.	Work with your child's teacher to establish expectations and consequences that are consistent between home and school.

Government Activities

1 | Rules at Home and Rules at School

Learning happens when: you and your child talk about rules. Why are they important? Ask your child to fold the piece of paper into three columns. Label the left one "Home," the right one "School," and the center one "Both." Brainstorm with your child the kinds of rules a person needs to follow at home. Don't fight? Put away toys and clothes? How about at school? Take turns? Don't push in line?

TIME: 20 minutes

MATERIALS

paper
pencils

Ask your child to write down where each rule belongs. Some rules may apply in both situations. Those will go in the middle column. Don't forget to talk with your child about how breaking a rule has consequences.

- Talk with your child about what rules adults have to follow. Are there house rules? Driving rules? Work rules? Does everyone have rules? What rules do the adults in your house have to follow?

- Ask your child to take a few sheets of paper and fold each in half. On one side, ask your child to write a rule such as, "Put away clean clothes." Then, have him illustrate the rule. On the other side of the paper, ask your child to draw a picture of what someone *not* following the rule would be doing.

- Help your child make a family rules poster to post in the house as a reminder to everyone. Sometimes children aren't the only ones who need a reminder of the rules.

Mastery occurs when: your child can identify rules for different situations.

You may want to help your child a little more if: he doesn't understand what rules are appropriate for different situations. Sometimes kids have trouble thinking of the rules on their own—they know what the rules are, but they need a little help vocalizing them. Start with basic rules that apply at home. Give your child two options and let him choose which one is correct. Then ask your child to write the correct one down in the home column. Continue until your child starts to think of some on his own, or until the page is complete.

2 Aye or Nay

TIME: 10 minutes

MATERIALS
▪ chalkboard or white-board
▪ chalk or whiteboard markers

Learning happens when: you talk with your child about fairness. What would she do if she and a group of friends needed to decide on what to do after school—play outside or play inside? How would she make a fair choice? What about a vote? Talk with your child about the voting process. Voting helps people make decisions that are fair to everyone involved.

Take a family vote on the evening meal. Let your child gather everyone together. Give your family two different dinner options and ask your child to write them on the board. As each family member makes his or her decision, let your child tally up the votes. Voilà! You know what you're making for dinner and your child learns a little bit about voting.

Variations: Try a secret ballot. Instead of announcing the results, let your child pass out paper and pencils. Each person should write his or her decision on the sheet of paper. Your child should tally up the votes and then announce the results.

Talk with your child about the importance of voting. Why should people vote? Why do you think some people don't vote? What might help them change their minds?

👁 During an election year, watch the election coverage with your child on television. Talk with your child about each of the candidates and what they stand for. On Election Day, help your child keep track of how each candidate is doing in the polls until the voting is over.

✋ Take your child with you the next time you go to vote. Explain who and what you are voting for and why. Show your child what the voting machine looks like and how it works.

Mastery occurs when: your child understands the concept of voting and how it helps make decisions fair.

You may want to help your child a little more if: she is confused by the voting process. Give your child a few examples of situations where voting would help resolve a situation. Ask her to try and think of a time when she would use a vote to resolve a situation.

3 | Flying High

Learning happens when: you show your child the American flag. If you don't have one, go somewhere such as your child's school or the local municipal building to see a flag. Find out how much your child knows about the flag. Who is believed to have made it? (Betsy Ross) When? (1776) What do the stars and stripes symbolize? (Stars are the fifty states, stripes are the thirteen original colonies)

Now it's your child's turn. Ask your child to imagine that he has been asked to design a flag for a new land. What things would he want symbolized in the new flag? What colors would he use? Help your child write out his ideas and then let him draw it.

TIME: 20 minutes

MATERIALS
- American flag
- pencils
- lined paper
- markers
- construction paper

Variations: Let your child create a family flag. Make sure to stress the symbolism that goes into the creation. Does your child's sibling love horses? Can it be incorporated somehow? Maybe the family vacations at the same favorite spot every year. See if your child can use that as an idea.

- After your child has created the flag for the new land, ask him to explain why he made it in the way that he did. What do the colors represent? What shapes did he decide on and why?

- Ask your child to cut out different colors of construction paper and glue the shapes to a larger piece of paper to make a flag.

- If you and your child are truly creative, go to the craft store and get the cloth and other materials to actually *make* a family flag to hang in the house.

Mastery occurs when: your child can comprehend the symbolism and importance of the flag.

You may want to help your child a little more if: he has trouble understanding the significance of the flag to American culture and the American people.

4 │ My Local Government

TIME: 30 minutes

MATERIALS
newspaper articles about local government

Learning happens when: you and your child read articles about local government. Ask your child to choose the article that most interests her. Then read aloud the article your child chose. Ask your child to clap her hands every time she hears a fact about the local government. Go back through the article with your child and make sure each clap she made was an actual fact.

Variations: To extend this activity, ask your child what part of government each fact relates to. For example, the speed limit relates to the police department, which is enforcing a law.

- Listen to a local news radio station broadcast with your child. After a few minutes, talk with your child about what you listened to. What parts dealt with the local government? How? What part of government?

- Give your child a chance to peruse your local newspaper for pictures that illustrate people, places, or events in your local government. Read the article that relates to the photo, then discuss why the newspaper might have chosen that particular picture.

- Make this activity more active for your kinesthetic learner by changing the clapping to a jumping jack or hopping on one foot.

Mastery occurs when: your child can identify information dealing with areas of the local government.

You may want to help your child a little more if: she is having difficulty picking out a fact versus an opinion. Choose an article that is mainly fact-based, such as one dealing with election results or other concrete information. The more fact-based the subject matter, the more comfortable your child will be in picking out the facts.

Geography

Is Istanbul Constantinople or is it the other way around? Where is Istanbul anyway? Are we there yet? After this section, on your next trip in the car with your child you can take along a map and help him or her track when you will get there and how long it will take. While children are learning about their own community, they are also learning where in the world it is. In second grade, oceans, continents, countries, and rivers are introduced to your child through maps. Your child will be learning how to read a map, use a compass, and use a key, and how maps help people locate places.

The following table describes some important concepts related to geography, where children can run into problems, and what you can do to help them along.

Geography Concepts	Having Problems?	Quick Tips
Knows cardinal directions and can name things on the north or west side of town.	Is unable to remember cardinal directions and has trouble naming things on the north or west side of town.	Talk about directions when driving around your town. Find a landmark that helps your child identify one of the cardinal directions (for example, the mountains are in the west or the water tower is north), then concentrate on that direction and its opposite (for example, east and west).
Names the seven continents.	Is unable to name the seven continents.	Memory, memory, memory! Use any device that works for your child and work on memorizing.
Is able to use the map key and other features to read a simple map.	Has trouble reading a simple map.	Draw maps every chance you get— simple maps from your house to the school or a friend's house— and gradually make the maps more detailed.

Geography Activities

1 The Whole World in Your Hand

Learning happens when: you and your child take a look at the globe. Ask your child to locate each of the continents. Which continent do you live on? Using the balloon and markers, help your child create his own globe. Blow up the balloon as round as it will go. Using the real globe as a reference, let your child draw the continents on the balloon and label each. Now your child has a fun globe of his own!

Variations: Add in the oceans. Throughout the course of the year your child will be learning all of the major oceans as well, and this is a great opportunity to practice.

TIME: 15 minutes

MATERIALS

▪ globe
▪ large round balloon
▪ markers

- Talk with your child about where each continent is on the globe. You may want to take the time to discuss the concept of Pangea with your child—the theory that the continents were all connected at one point in time. Why might scientists think that? Do the continents look like they could have been connected? Why or why not? How do you think the continents ended up where they are now?

- Ask your child to draw in features like the Rocky Mountains or the Mississippi River.

- Try papier mâché and let your child get messy and creative. Use the blown-up balloon as a mold for the papier mâché. When it's dry, ask your child to draw the continents on the papier mâché, along with any other distinguishing features. When he is done, pop the balloon inside and pull it out. Voilà—instant globe!

Mastery occurs when: your child can identify and draw the continents of the world.

You may want to help your child a little more if: he is having trouble identifying the continents and where they are in the world. Start off with North America and South America. Then move to the next closest continent so that your child can identify which continent is found where on the globe.

2 | Pin the Continent on the World

TIME: 15 minutes

MATERIALS
shapes of continents and oceans (you can find them at www.knowledgeessentials.com)
large laminated sheet of poster board with the continents and oceans outlined on it (you can find self-laminating kits at your local office supply store)
nontoxic glue
velcro strips
cut-out, laminated, and labeled continents
blindfold
whiteboard markers

Tack or tape the poster board to the wall. Glue one side of the Velcro strip on each spot for the continents. Glue the other half on each of the continent shapes. Make sure you match them up correctly before securing the velcro.

Learning happens when: you give your child one of the shapes. Ask her to identify the continent and then to concentrate on the map for a minute. Blindfold your child and have her try to stick the continent where it belongs. Continue until all the continents are on the map.

Variations: Add in the oceans! After your child places all the continents on the map, give her a whiteboard marker and let her write in where each ocean belongs.

- Instead of blindfolding your child, give her hints as to where that continent might belong. For example, for Asia you could mention it's the biggest and that it's on the eastern side of the map.

- Instead of starting with the labeled continents, ask your child to begin this activity by identifying each continent and then writing the name of it on the shape with a marker.

👋 Ask your child to help you make the poster and continent shapes. You'll probably want to make the actual poster part yourself, but your child can help cut out the shapes and add the Velcro and names.

Mastery occurs when: your child can identify each continent and its proper place on the map.

You may want to help your child a little more if: she has trouble identifying where the continents go on the map. Forget the blindfold. Let your child look at the map until she can place each piece correctly a few times.

3 | Which Way to Go

Learning happens when: you talk with your child about directions. Show your child the map and ask which way is north. South? East? West? How do you know? Put the map away and then take a walk outside. Ask your child again to point out the four directions. How do you know? Explain that a compass can help in figuring out which way a person is headed, how the arrow in the compass always points north, and how you can figure out the other directions based on just one. Go for a walk with your child and let him navigate the way.

Variations: Map out a little path for your child to follow. Ask your child to use the compass to fill in the directions.

👂 Go to a large field with your child and let him carry the compass. Start off going north and then shout out a different direction you'd like to go in, letting your child figure out which way you need to go. Continue until you get to the other side of the field. Don't forget to ask your child how he knows which direction is correct.

TIME: Varies

MATERIALS
- map of your town
- compass

👁 Get a local map and mark out a path for your child, making sure it has quite a few twists and turns. Ask your child to use the compass to figure out what directions he would need to go, and then write out the directions on a sheet of paper.

✋ Go for a nature hike on a local trail. Before leaving, get a map of the trail and ask your child to use the compass and plan a course for the way there and for the way back.

Mastery occurs when: your child knows what a compass is for and how to use it.

You may want to help your child a little more if: he is having difficulty using the compass to find north. Give your child the compass and ask him to turn slowly around halfway while watching the needle of the compass. Explain that he is in the opposite direction, south, but the needle is still in the same spot, pointing north. No matter where your child turns, the needle will always point north. Have your child continue turning until the *N* is under the point of the needle. That's how you use a compass to find north. Now ask him to locate the other directions.

4 | Bird's-Eye View

Learning happens when: you place a few small objects in a box. Place the box on the floor and ask your child to stand up and look into the box. Ask your child to identify what the objects are. Talk with your child about how different they look at such a height. Show your child the map and explain that it is an overhead view, as if she were standing over something like the box. Point out the key on the side of the map. What do the symbols stand for? Ask your child to compare the key to the different symbols on the map.

Ask your child to imagine what her room would look like as an overhead map. What important things would need to be in the key? A bed? A dresser? A desk? What about a closet? What shapes would you use to symbolize them? Help your child create an overhead map of her room, and don't forget the key!

Variations: Let your child create a city or room out of building blocks. Ask your child to stand over it and draw an overhead map.

- Ask your child to explain her key and overhead map to you when it's done. Talk with your child about how a map is useful for getting around a new place.

- Try this activity on a larger scale. Ask your child to make an overhead map of where you live, starting with your house. What are the nearby streets (if she doesn't remember, go outside with her and look). What important features are on your block? How about plants and trees? See how much your child can figure out on her own and then go around the neighborhood with her to see if there are other things that should go on the overhead map.

- Make a mini version of your child's room using a shoebox and dollhouse pieces. If your child is really creative, have her make the pieces of the room. Then ask your child to draw an overhead map to go with it.

Mastery occurs when: your child can read an overhead map and use the key.

You may want to help your child a little more if: she is not grasping the concept of a key. Show your child a few overhead maps without the keys and ask her what the shapes are. Try to find some maps that make it more difficult to distinguish what the symbols are. After letting your child guess for a while, bring out the key and let her use it to figure out what the shapes represent.

TIME: 30 minutes

MATERIALS
- few small objects
- box
- map with an overhead view of buildings and a key (such as a map of an amusement park or a zoo)
- paper
- pencils
- ruler
- crayons

5 Tasty State

TIME: 30–45 minutes

MATERIALS
- outline of your state (you can print one from www. knowledgeessentials.com)
- cookie dough
- various edible decorations (for example, candies and sprinkles)
- icing
- food coloring
- bowls
- popsicle sticks

Learning happens when: you ask your child to describe what your state looks like. Ask him to outline the state in the air. How accurate was it? Take out the outline of the state and let your child trace it with his finger to practice the shape.

Give your child the cookie dough and let him mold it into the shape of your state. Bake the shape and then let your child use the decorations to mark important features, such as the capital, mountains, or your house. Use the food coloring to make colored icing for land and water. Let your child get as creative as possible!

Variations: Bake a cake and make more states! Bake a cake in a 13 × 9 inch pan and let your child decorate it with not only the state you live in, but also the states that surround it.

- While you and your child are creating the state, talk with him about the nearby states. What are they shaped like? How do those states help shape your state?

- If your child is a visual learner, give him a laminated, enlarged photocopy of your state to form the cookie dough on. This will help him see exactly how the state is shaped.

- If you don't want to make an edible state, try using Play-doh. Use sequins, beads, string, and other decorative items to mark the important features.

Mastery occurs when: your child can correctly identify and replicate the shape of the state he lives in.

You may want to help your child a little more if: he can't identify the shape of his state. Practice with a jigsaw puzzle of the fifty states. Take your state and two other states and let your child pick out which one you live in. Mix them up with more states, or take away your state and see if your child notices.

Environmental Learning

Where do you live? Which town, which county, which state, and which country is your house in? Do you live by an ocean? By the Canadian or Mexican border? Talk about it! While driving, ask your child to help you navigate your way home from school. Point out important local government buildings. Take a walk around your community. Take your child with you to the voting booth. Read the newspaper with your child (something other than the funnies).

The greatest thing about social studies is that it is about the world around you, so there are plenty of opportunities to talk about it and experience it. There's only one way to diagram a sentence, but time is always moving and things are always happening. Use every chance you get to explore the world with your child.

End of Second Grade Social Studies Checklist

Students who are working on the standard level at the end of second grade:

_____ Know the name of the president of the United States

_____ Know some of the jobs the president does

_____ Know what state they live in and where it is in the country

_____ Know how to use a map and a key

_____ Can identify the seven continents

Teaching Your Second Grader Thinking Skills

10

Teaching your second grader to think sounds like a lofty goal, doesn't it? You can help foster a thinking mind in your child by treating him or her as an active participant in a home where you explore "why" and "how" questions. The more opportunities your child has to explore ideas and be heard at home, the more likely he or she is to be an active thinker both in and out of school.

Teaching children to think reasonably and logically improved children's impulsive behavior and social adjustment. These children were less likely to develop behavioral difficulties than were well-adjusted children who did not learn these skills. Of course, the way you respond to your child and act in front of him or her makes the largest impact on how your child learns to think and communicate.

In a study of children from kindergarten through fourth grade (Shure, 1993) that was the culmination of twenty years of research to test ideas about thinking skills, parent modeling, and behavior,

---

Beginning of Second Grade Thinking Skills Checklist

Students who are working at the standard level at the beginning of second grade:

____ Shift from learning through observation and experience to learning via language and logic

____ Demonstrate a longer attention span

____ Use serious, logical thinking; are thoughtful and reflective

____ Are able to understand reasoning and make decisions

M. B. Shure delineated four levels of communication that we use all the time:

LEVEL 1: POWER ASSERTION (DEMANDS, BELITTLES, PUNISHES)

- Do it because I say so!
- Do you want a time out?
- How many times have I told you . . . !
- If you can't share the truck, I'll take it away so that neither of you will have it.

LEVEL 2: POSITIVE ALTERNATIVE (NO EXPLANATION)

- I'm on the phone now. Go watch TV.
- Ask him for the truck.
- You should share your toys.

LEVEL 3: INDUCTION (EXPLANATIONS AND REASONS)

- I feel angry when you interrupt me.
- If you hit, you'll lose a friend (hurt him).
- You'll make him angry if you hit him (grab toys).
- You shouldn't hit (grab). It's not nice.

LEVEL 4: PROBLEM-SOLVING PROCESS (TEACHING THINKING)

- What's the problem? What's the matter?
- How do you think I (she/he) feel(s) when you hit (grab)?
- What happened (might happen) when you did (do) that?
- Can you think of a different way to solve this problem (tell him/her/me how you feel)?
- Do you think that is or is not a good idea? Why (why not)?

The parents who communicated as often as possible on level 4 in Shure's study had children who were the least impulsive, the least withdrawn, and showed the fewest behavior problems as observed by independent raters.

We all know that there are times when communicating on level 1 is the only way to go, so don't beat yourself up. You can't reason a child out of the street when a car is coming. Awareness of the communication levels enables you to implement the highest level as much of the time as possible, which in turn fosters a thinking child.

Teaching and modeling thinking encourages children to ask questions of information and ideas. It helps your child learn how to identify unstated assumptions, form and defend opinions, and see relationships between events and ideas. A thinking person raises a thinking child. That you are even reading this assures that you are a thinking person, so you are on the right track.

Don't expect for your child's first grade teacher to stand up in front of class and say "Okay, it's time to learn to think." Instead, your child's teacher will incorporate activities and language that foster the development and refinement of thinking skills, such as problem solving, concentration, and reasoning, throughout your child's daily activities. In the same way, you will foster thinking skills if you do many of the activities in this book with your child.

There are many approaches to teaching thinking. You can teach your child to use a set of identifiable skills, such as deciding between relevant and irrelevant information and generating questions from written material. This is particularly useful for auditory and visual learners. Your kinesthetic child learns to think more actively by participating in sports, hands-on projects, and other similar activities.

Problem Solving

Problem solving is a hallmark of mathematical activity and a major means of developing mathematical knowledge. It is finding a way to reach a goal that is not immediately attainable. Problem solving is natural to young children because the world is new to them, and they exhibit curiosity, intelligence, and flexibility as they face new situations. The challenge at this level is to build on children's innate problem-solving inclinations and to preserve and encourage a disposition that values problem solving. Try the problem-solving math section in chapter 7 and the science activities about systems in chapter 8 as challenging opportunities for your child.

Concentration

Thinking skills begin with the ability to maintain a focus on one thing long enough to think it through. Thinking something through means understanding the information (in whatever form—for example, visual, print, or oral), questioning the information, and thinking about the alternatives before making a decision.

Concentration skills are a big part of learning to read. Your child's teacher will be working hard with him or her on concentration skills, and you can help reinforce these skills by trying the activities in the reading comprehension section of chapter 5.

Comprehension

This is a hard one. To think about something in a reasonable, logical manner, you need to understand it, but creative thinking is born from instances where you don't understand something. The trick is probably in the mix. Let your child explore new information and form creative thoughts about it, then talk to him or her logically about it. Giving your child time to think freely about new information allows him or her to think about it in many contexts and many forms before being told which concept or form is proper.

In order to better develop your child's understanding of different concepts, his or her perception should be shaped by touching, hearing, and seeing something simultaneously, to experience the concept as best as he or she can. Take time to let your child talk about what he or she is seeing, touching, and hearing. By experiencing new concepts in different contexts, your child can become aware of different aspects of an idea and develop his or her understanding of its meaning.

Reasoning

There is more than one type of reasoning. Formal reasoning skills, such as deductive and inductive reasoning, are developed at a later age. The reasoning skill that is focused on in second grade is spatial-temporal reasoning, or the ability to visualize and transform objects in space.

Spatial-temporal operations are responsible for combining separate elements of an object into a single whole, or for arranging objects in a specific spatial order. Spatial-temporal operations require successive steps; each step is dependent on previous ones.

Spatial-temporal skills are the most frequently tested reasoning/thinking skills on IQ and other standardized tests. You can work on these skills with your child through the math and science activities in this book.

Logic

Children learn about and understand logical concepts in different ways. In math, for example, some kids think about numbers in terms of where they are on a number line, while other kids think about how many objects make up each number. These children reach an understanding of numbers, their meaning, and how to use them, but they reach it in different ways. Taking this example further, these children comprehend the information and understand what numbers represent. But if one group is then asked to handle the numbers in different contexts, the group will need to be aware of different aspects of numbers in order to develop a fuller understanding of their meaning. The group can then think about numbers in different ways and apply them to different situations in a logical way rather than simply recall what they mean.

A large part of logical thinking stems from the ability to see objects and apply concepts in many contexts (spatial-temporal reasoning applies here). Teaching children to question information teaches them to think about the information in more than one context before making a logical conclusion about it. Logical thinking can be reinforced during the discipline process by applying logical consequences to a behavior rather than using an arbitrary punishment.

Thinking Skills Activities

To help your child develop thinking skills, you can:

- Encourage her to ask questions about the world around her.

- Ask him to imagine what will happen next in the story when you are reading together.

- Actively listen to your child's conversation, responding seriously and nonjudgmentally to her questions.

- Ask what he is feeling and why when he expresses feelings.

- Suggest that she find facts to support her opinions, and encourage her to locate information relevant to her opinions.

- Use entertainment—a book, a TV program, or a movie—as the basis of family discussions.

- Use daily activities as occasions for learning (environmental learning).

- Reward him for inquisitive and/or creative activity that is productive.

- Ask her what she learned at school.

Environmental Learning

There are thousands of ways that you can use your child's everyday environment to encourage thinking skills. Remember, if your child is an active participant in a home where there are "why" and "how" discussions, he or she is more likely to be an active thinker both in and out of school.

End of Second Grade Thinking Skills Checklist

Students who are working on the standard level at the end of second grade:

____ Start to use symbolic reasoning to complement more concrete manipulations

____ Draw inferences

____ Differentiate between fact and opinion

____ Try to find answers to self-generated questions

____ Draw conclusions

Assessment

11

A key component to learning is evaluating what has been learned. Assessment serves several different purposes:

1. Assessing individual student abilities and knowledge and adapting instructions accordingly

2. Evaluating and improving the instructional program in general

3. Determining individual student eligibility for promotion or graduation, college admission, or special honors

4. Measuring and comparing school, school district, statewide, and national performance for broad public accountability

There is more than one kind of assessment and more than one context in which this term is frequently used. There are multiple ways that you and your child's teacher assess your child. There is broad assessment of your child's knowledge of certain things and his performance as compared to other children of the same age and grade. Standardized assessment is usually done at the end of the year and comprises many sessions of test taking in a short time period. There are uses for all types of assessment.

Assessing Individual Student Abilities and Knowledge

Students learn in different ways, so teachers assess their daily learning in different ways. The most common way to assess daily learning is by observing how your child responds to and implements things that he or she learns in the classroom. As teachers observe and consider the variety of daily assignments of students, they begin to help their students demonstrate this learning on tests.

Observation and Portfolio Assessment

Your child's overall progress is assessed by considering her developmental stage and cognitive learning abilities with key concepts and key skills within the framework of her learning styles. Teachers (and by now, you) do this by observing your child on a daily basis, giving basic skills tests, gauging reaction and comprehension time when given new information, and asking frequent, informal questions. All of the activities in this book include explanations for how to assess your child's performance, and the checklists at the beginning and end of the chapters can help you assess your child's progress in each skill.

Teachers have begun to implement portfolio assessment more frequently. Teachers are giving your child the opportunity to demonstrate learning through a variety of activities, such as art projects, writing activities, oral presentations, and daily participation with unit tests, to determine the true levels of comprehension and skill development with the variety of materials and skills in each learning unit. Many people think portfolio assessment is one of the most accurate methods of determining learning, but it can be subjective, so it has been criticized. Teachers try really hard not to be subjective; contrary to what some people think, they aren't likely to retaliate for a mishap with a parent by lowering the child's grades. When a child succeeds, the teacher has also succeeded. Discounting the child's success because of personal feelings destroys the teacher's professional success.

Always remember (even if your child does really well) that achievement tests are just one measure of your child's learning. You know this is true because you have been using rough measures in the activities you do with your child. Observation is a primary assessment tool.

Standardized Testing

Testing is a hot topic, and rightly so. We all remember the standardized tests—spending days filling in little circles with a number 2 pencil.

The majority of teachers dislike standardized testing for a number of reasons. Sure, there is the issue of accountability. But the heart of the issue is not that teachers are afraid of being held to a standard to keep their job—it is that they disagree with being held to what many of them believe is a false standard. Think about how an auditory or physical learner will do on a test designed for visual learners. The tests aren't an accurate picture of what all learners can do.

In defense of test makers, they are doing their best to adjust their approaches within the limitations of state requirements, logistical requirements, and traditional business practices. But the system within which teachers, parents, students, and test makers are trying to operate is definitely imperfect.

Others' issues are centered around "teaching the test." Teachers are afraid the curriculum they are told to teach will be so narrowly geared toward the test that it will limit their ability to teach the things that support the tested items. They are concerned they will only be able to teach to the cognitive learning level when they know the student should also be able to apply the knowledge, synthesize it, and evaluate it. We have discussed how individual scores can be invalid, but so can group scores. Test results may be invalidated by teaching so narrowly to the objectives of a particular test that scores are raised without actually improving the broader, often more important, set of academic skills that the test should be measuring.

At the end of the day, assessment is a very strong tool. It encourages, discourages, and measures learning. Assessment should be a means of fostering growth toward high expectations and should support student learning. When assessments are used in thoughtful and meaningful ways and combined with information from other sources, students' scores provide important information that can lead to decisions that promote student learning and equality of opportunity. The misuse of tests for high-stakes purposes (tests that are used to make significant educational decisions about children, teachers, schools, or school districts) has undermined the benefits these tests can foster.

The standardized tests that cause so much controversy are norm-referenced tests, meaning the test questions are selected so that a national sample of students' test scores will result in a normal distribution: there will always be a group of students at the bottom, a majority in the middle, and a group at the top. It is unrealistic to expect whole groups of students to be in the top percentiles (or groups) on these tests. Most students are expected to perform near the fiftieth percentile.

Helping Your Child Test Well

You play a vital role in helping your child succeed on standardized tests. Here are just a few things you can do:

- Put your child at ease by discussing your own experiences with taking tests. If you were nervous or anxious, talk about it. Let him know those feelings are normal.

- Be aware of the specific days tests will be given. Ask your child how the testing sessions are going. Offer encouragement.

- Stress the importance of listening to test directions and following them carefully. Provide practice activities at home, such as following a recipe or reading and answering questions about a story.

- Make sure your child goes to bed early every night and at the same time every night, especially on the night before testing.

- Encourage healthy eating, rest, and exercise.

- Most standardized testing is given over a three- or four-day period. Ask your child's teacher for a schedule, and make sure your child attends school on those days.

- Meet with your child's teachers to discuss the results. If your child had difficulty in specific areas, ask teachers for suggestions in the form of homework assignments, techniques, and specific material.

What the Scores Really Mean

High-stakes tests are used to make significant educational decisions about children, teachers, schools, or school districts. To use a single objective test in the determination of such things as graduation, course credit, grade placement, promotion to the next grade, or placement in special groups is a serious misuse of tests. Remember, your child's score on a standardized test is only one measure of what he knows. Most schools use multiple measures, including student projects, homework, portfolios, chapter tests, and oral reports.

Measuring and Comparing School, School District, Statewide, and National Performance for Broad Public Accountability

Increasingly, policy makers at the federal, state, and local levels want to identify ways to measure student performance in order to see how well the public education system is doing its job. The goals of this accountability approach include providing information about the status of the educational system, motivating desired change, measuring program effectiveness, and creating systems for rewarding and sanctioning educators based on the performance of their students.

The use of testing to change classroom instruction is central to the theory of standards-based reform. It assumes that educators and the public can agree on what should be taught; that a set of clear standards can be developed, which in turn drive curriculum and instruction; and that tests can measure how well students perform based on those standards.

Second Grade Society   12

Kindergarten and first grade were really good for getting you and your child acclimated to the playground. That is a big step, so pat yourself on the back. You aren't home free, but you are at least on second base. Understanding the social structure of school isn't hard—we all remember how it was. The good part is that elementary school is still pretty loose. Kids will pick their favorite friends but they are usually still open to doing things with all children. Still, you are worried—your baby is playing on *teams*, you keep finding weird things in his or her pockets, and there is evidence that you may, in fact, have raised a whiner. Let's talk about second grade society.

Second Grade Social Development

Whether your child learns at private school, public school, or home, here are some characteristics of your second grader's social development:

- Increasing independence is characteristic of all ages, but you will see a jump here.

- Your child will want to do things by and for him- or herself, but still needs adults who will help when asked or when needed.

- Second graders are still likely to be friends with the same sex and those friends:

  Provide fun and excitement through play.

  Facilitate learning by watching and talking to one another.

  Assist in times of trouble by banding together.

  Give support in times of stress.

  Help your child understand how he or she feels about him- or herself

- Your child can see things from another child's point of view, but still has trouble understanding the feelings and needs of other people.

- Many times your child might need help to express his or her feelings in appropriate ways when upset or worried.

- A second grader can carry criticism too long.

Enough generalizations; let's get down to some serious personality and activity issues.

The Three-Headed Second Grade Control Freak

Have you ever sent your child to school wearing shorts in February because it was the easiest thing to do? Does your eight-year-old's behavior rule from the dinner table to what will be watched on TV? Step away from the child. Take a look at him or her. Listen, really listen. Admit to yourself that you serve macaroni six days a week because your child will ruin the meal if you don't.

The Picky Eater

Popular convention says that a picky eater is seeking attention. The child is controlling the dinner hour, requesting specific sack lunches and refusing to eat cafeteria food. Picky eaters are so misunderstood. Is it a power play? Perhaps, but only after power is exerted upon the eater—to make him or her eat what he or she does not want. This may seem radical, but perhaps this control issue arises only after what the child sees as instigation.

Does picky eating occur because of your child's desire to control mealtime? Maybe, but that will go away. We are talking about chronic, spit it out or throw it up, I can't eat that to save my life picky eating. Will your child put him- or herself through that as part of some psycho-child head trip on you?

Let's think about this, though: nutrition is a pretty hard concept to grasp for grown-ups, let alone an eight-year-old. So the likelihood of your little one hatching a master plan to eat the same thing over and over just to make you mad isn't high. Yes, he or she may do it a few times to see your funny reaction, but that gets old, too. All your child really knows is that he or she is supposed to eat or not eat, or drink or not drink, something because it is good or bad for him or her.

Now, do you think your child has heard you say that you don't like to eat something? Your child hears you say that you like or don't like certain foods, and guess what? Your child also likes and dislikes certain foods. Can you hear your child saying "Why can you say no if you don't like it but I can't?" and the power struggle ensues when the only issue was over what tasted good.

Now you have a choice: do you enter into a power play with an eight-year-old or do you outwit him or her? The more successful choice is to outwit:

Step 1: Hold your breath, count to ten, and ignore.

Step 2: Offer your child choices regarding mealtime instead of just regarding the food—what plates to use, what drinks to have, the conversation, and so on.

Step 3: Include one thing you know your child likes at each meal, including sack lunches.

The truth is that if your child has truly sensitive taste buds, this problem is not going away anytime soon. Help your child learn how to pick out new things that are similar to what he or she already likes. As the years go by, talk to him or her about the embarrassment of sitting at a fancy dinner and not eating a thing because the food looks funny. If he or she doesn't learn to expand his or her palate, your child will at least get some coping mechanisms that allow him or her to eat in a wide variety of settings.

The Whiner

There's a recessive gene present in all children, and most certainly inherited from your mate: the whining gene. The little darlings know how to manipulate behavior with speech. Dealing with a whiner is a slippery slope. Dealing with it effectively will make your child much more likable to you and others. Dealing with it ineffectively will make it worse.

Manipulator or Dying to Be Heard?

Children whine to annoy adults, right? Wrong. Children whine to manipulate behavior and/or to be heard. The keys to ending this lie in figuring out why your child is whining and then choosing a method to deal with it that fits both of your personalities. Try one or a combination of these.

For mini manipulators:

1. No habla whining. Act as if your child is speaking a foreign language anytime he or she whines. "What did you say? I am so sorry, I don't understand whining."

2. Benevolent dictatorship. Your household is not a democracy. You are the boss, so be the boss. Let your "no" mean no and your "yes" mean yes. Giving in to whining just perpetuates the habit.

3. Good for the goose. If your child whines, whine right back. *Do not cross the line of mocking your child or being mean.* This is a playful

approach and you will know if this method is appropriate for you and your child.

For some children, whining is a way of saying "Hear me, please hear me!"

1. The well-reasoned child (dying to be heard). Calmly but firmly explain to your child why whining is not appropriate (it's annoying, manipulative, repulsive, and so on). Help your child identify times when he or she is whining by pointing it out in a consistent and firm manner.

2. Look and listen before you leap. Is your child whining because you aren't really listening to what he or she really has to say? Is it the only way your child can get your attention? Try fixing that before getting too angry with your child.

3. Oh, drama! Is your child *always* dying to be heard? Have you ever seen one child emote *so* much? Is "Look at me, Mom!" heard second only to "Listen to me, Dad!" in your house? You have a drama king or queen and whining is his or her latest trick. Ignore the whining and talk to your child about how no one likes excessive drama about things in daily life.

4. It's just the way I talk. Some people like being the "baby" and speak in a high-pitched and whiny voice. It can become a habit. Watch out for it and nip it in the bud. Address any other underlying issues and give your child loving reinforcement for appropriate behaviors.

The Good Sport

Team sports begin to take on a life of their own by second grade. Soccer, soccer, soccer. Basketball, baseball, and softball, oh my! How are you going to work this into your and your child's schedule? Do you really have to go to every game where the talking lady who saves you a seat at *every* game will always be sitting right by you? Yes, you do.

As a former coach, I have some things to say in favor of team sports. Being a part of a team teaches children to:

- Value giving their best effort
- Interact with groups
- Follow the rules of the game
- Be a good winner and a good loser
- Know that they can count on others to do their jobs
- Know that others depend on them to do their job
- Practice, practice, practice
- Be disciplined
- Respect what their bodies can physically accomplish

It is true that you need to be cautious about overscheduling events in your child's life. It is also true that your child should be given the opportunity to try lots of different things to find what he or she is truly interested in continuing. Even if your child finds that music, dance, or some other activity best suits him or her, there is great value to at one point excessively encourage your child to play team sports. Particularly at this age, it is a great time in your child's developmental stage to introduce the concepts associated with being on a team. Kids whose parents actively encourage their physical pursuits—by driving them to soccer practice, say, and cheering them on—are much more likely to stick with these activities than kids whose parents show little enthusiasm.

The main focus at this age is making fitness fun and developing skills, not producing future Olympians or beating the other team. You don't want to pressure your child to perform or force him or her to do a sport he or she doesn't like. Both strategies almost always backfire, and you risk turning your child away from physical activity altogether. Whether your child chooses an organized sport, which can teach leadership and teamwork skills along with improving overall fitness and motor skills, or a solo pursuit, which can also foster self-sufficiency, focus on having fun and developing skills.

Let's talk about some other important aspects of team sports, such as losing and winning.

Losing

How does your child handle losing? Is it a direct reflection of how *you* handle losing? Realizing loss with grace and dignity begins now and is one of the most valuable lessons your child may gain from competition. The first thing to do is check yourself and make sure you are modeling the behavior you want your child to emulate. If you aren't, then start now.

Here are some ways you can help your child learn to lose well:

- Play on your child's sense of empathy. At this age, he is starting to develop the ability to put himself in another person's place. He can now begin to understand that getting angry when he doesn't win hurts the feelings of the people that he is playing with. Ask your child to think about how it would feel if someone got angry at him when he did something he was proud of. Tell your child that it's okay to be sad about losing, but he should try not to hurt others because of it.

- Mix in cooperative games. Noncompetitive games eliminate winning and losing altogether and help your child learn what it's like to play on a team. Try playing a game of Chinese checkers in which the idea is to get your marbles on her side and hers on your side at roughly the same time.

- Emphasize effort, skill, and fun. It's trite but true: it's not whether you win or lose but how you play the game. Your job is to get your child to take this adage to heart. After he plays a game with a friend, ask, "Did you have a good time?" instead of, "Who won?"

Offer praise for anything done well, no matter how small it may seem. The more you can get your child thinking about developing the skills needed to be a good player—regardless of the outcome—the less important winning becomes.

Winning

How does your child handle winning? Is it a direct reflection of how *you* handle winning? Winning with grace and dignity begins now and may be more important than losing with grace and dignity. Gloating, bragging, and making fun of others is not appealing on any level, and it is never too early to instill this in your child. The following are several ways to help your child be a good winner:

- Give your child opportunities to lose as she plays against you. It seems harsh, but don't always let your child win. Your child won't improve at a sport if she isn't sufficiently challenged.

- Most important, don't let your child see you being a poor sport. Take your losses well, and always congratulate the winner.

- Show your child what it means to be a good winner as well. Good winners don't brag about victories or make fun of another player's skills.

Cheating

We all want our children to succeed, but not if it means cheating. To quash the rule-breaker in your child, try these tips:

- Use empathy. Explain to your child that when he does not follow the rules, the other players feel bad. Remind him that if everyone cheated, playing would be no fun at all.

- Cheaters never win. Make it clear that cheating cancels out winning. If your child changes the way the dice roll when you are playing with her, for example, explain that this may be effective for getting the most points, but she isn't winning because she isn't following the rules. Taking away the reward for cheating takes away the desire to cheat.

- Emphasize that the fun lies in the playing, not in the winning. We've all heard this before, but that's because it's true. The easiest way to drive this point home is to teach by example: if you lose, don't lament the fact that you lost; instead, say what a great time you had playing. And during a game, don't say things like "I hope I win" or "Oh, no, I'm behind." Instead of thinking about the outcome, stay focused on what you and your child are doing in the present. Phrases like "That was a smart move" or "What a lucky roll!" help keep children engaged in the fun of the moment.

- Find ways to help your child feel competent in other areas of his life. Praise his ability to ride a bike, for instance, or admire his growing skill with drawing. The more confident your child is in general, the less he will feel the need to win (and cheat, if necessary) to build self-esteem.

If you do catch your child cheating, don't overreact, and don't call him or her a cheater. Calmly let your child know that what he or she is doing isn't fair and that he or she must follow the rules of the game. You want your child to develop a conscience, not think he or she is a bad person.

Money Money Money Money

Eight-year-olds have figured out that money has a value and buys the things they want. They get money for doing chores, lost teeth, and birthdays, and if you are late on any payments the gifted eight-year-old will calculate the interest. If your child has his or her own money, it usually doesn't matter if you like what he or she wants to buy—it is his or her money. Your child likes that.

Counting money is a pretty big topic in math during the first and second grades. Economic concepts—such as unlimited wants and limited resources—have been introduced in social studies and your child experiences these concepts every time he or she goes to the store with you. Your child has probably started participating in fundraising activities at school. Money is one concept that kids take from knowledge straight through to synthesis without a second thought.

Your child's familiarity with money-related concepts isn't the worst thing in the world. This is a good time for you to start a savings account in your child's name, unless you already have. Maintain the bank book together. Set savings goals such as for college but also for a new bike perhaps, and your child will be on the right financial path.

Money can be a really good incentive for children, even at this age, except for grades. It is bad form to pay your child a certain amount for each A and B. Try using money to motivate your child to do the things that people really get paid for—like chores, lawn work, baby-sitting, and cooking—not for learning or for doing things that your child should have the strength of character to do anyway.

Moving On to Third Grade

You made it! Your second grader is now going to be a third grader, and you are going to be the parent of a third grader!

You can monitor your child's readiness for third grade and determine areas that you can help your child reinforce with the following subject area and developmental checklists.

Ready to Go

Students who are ready to go on to third grade:

Reading

____ Read with understanding and fluency

____ Figure out unknown words in context

____ Recognize word patterns (prefixes and suffixes)

____ Communicate in writing

____ Retell stories with accuracy

____ Correct themselves while reading

____ Identify and spell many words

____ Recognize parts of a story

____ Read for more than pleasure

____ Use a larger sight vocabulary

Writing

____ Write about their own ideas

____ Pick out nouns and verbs in sentences

____ Explain the problem, solution, or main idea in fiction and nonfiction

____ Revise their writing to make it clearer

____ Read and understand stories, poems, plays, directories, newspapers, charts, and diagrams

____ Write different types of sentences

Math

____ Add and subtract two-and-three-digit numbers

____ Collect and compare seasonal temperatures using a thermometer

____ Use time to sequence events of the day

____ Recognize, identify, and create a circle, a quadrilateral, a rhombus, a square, a triangle, a trapezoid, a hexagon, and a parallelogram

____ Compare and contrast the characteristics of shapes

____ Model and find the perimeter of simple shapes

_____ Estimate and measure length, weight, and capacity using standard units of measurement

_____ Use appropriate tools and terms to explore measurement

Science

_____ Identify various constellations

_____ Can associate Earth's axis and orbit with seasonal changes

_____ Identify the nine planets

_____ Understand the importance of exercise and a good diet for a healthy body

_____ Recognize different types of clouds and the weather they predict

_____ Can explain the importance of the senses

Social Studies

_____ Know the name of the president of the United States

_____ Know some of the jobs the president does

_____ Know what state they live in and where it is in the country

_____ Know how to use a map and a key

_____ Can identify the seven continents

Thinking

_____ Start to use symbolic reasoning to complement more concrete manipulations

_____ Draw inferences

____ Differentiate between fact and opinion

____ Ttry to find answers to self-generated questions

____ Draw conclusions

Anxieties

There are always going to be anxieties when moving on to another grade. After all, you just got to know the second grade teacher and you really like her. Who will be the homeroom mom next year? Wait—this is supposed to be about the children's anxieties, right? Wrong. Everyone is going to feel a little sad, a little anxious, a little excited, and really glad it is summer when the subject of third grade arises.

Minimizing "Brain Drain"

Now that your child has acquired tangible skills that are building blocks for future learning, you are facing your second year of the challenge of keeping those skills fresh. Here are some things to keep in mind to help your child retain his or her second grade skills during the summer months.

Do

- Reinforce skills from his or her second grade year through environmental learning.
- Go to the library on a regular basis.
- Include learning activities in your weekly summer routine.
- Encourage free and creative thinking through art projects or active play.

DON'T

- Try to "get ahead" for the next year.

- Have your child spend the whole summer with a tutor.

- Ignore obvious learning opportunities (such as mapping out the trip to Grandma's).

Your child's second grade year has been enhanced, supported, and furthered by your efforts. Continue creating the learning environment that you worked so hard on this year over the summer and into third grade. You are on the right track.

LITERATURE FOR SECOND GRADERS

This section contains a list of books that your child may find interesting and learning activities along with the reading selections. You can find more recommended literature for your second grader at www.knowledgeessentials.com.

Stone Soup

Author: Heather Forest
Publisher: August House

This book, of which there are many variations, follows two travelers who are denied food by a village. They trick the people into making "stone soup" and convince them to add ingredients to make it taste better. The moral of this story is sharing.

Special Considerations: This book includes great pictures of each ingredient that help children identify words with pictures.

Learning: Discuss the importance of sharing. Talk about the types of food that the townspeople share with the travelers. Look up information on food groups.

Activity: Ask your child to create his own recipe for stone stoup. If it's an edible creation, have him help you make it for dinner.

Follow-Up: Discuss the food groups with your child and differentiate between healthy food versus unhealthy food choices.

Morris the Moose Goes to School
Author: Bernard Wiseman
Publisher: Scholastic

This book is about a moose who decides to go to school to learn how to read and count. After going to school, Morris is able to read store signs and count his money to buy gumdrops.

Special Considerations: This is a book your child will love to read on her own. It is something she can relate to and will enjoy.

Learning: Talk about why Morris the Moose needs to go to school. What important things did he learn how to do?

Activity: Make a list with your child of things she doesn't know how to do. Brainstorm ways to learn about them. What can your child learn in school? From you? From books?

Follow-Up: Pick a topic that your child can learn from a book. Go to the library and check out a book to help her research the topic.

Young Cam Jansen and the Dinosaur Game
Author: David A. Adler
Publisher: Puffin

Cam Jansen and her friend Eric are invited to a birthday party that becomes the stage for a mystery. Cam gets suspicious when one party guest is able to guess the exact number of dinosaurs in a jar. She follows the clues to figure things out.

Special Considerations: This is one book in a series of Cam Jansen mysteries by this author. If this book seems too much of a challenge for your child, you can get an easier one to start with.

Learning: This book is a good example of following clues, or directions, to reach a goal. Talk with your child about how following directions can help get things done. How do directions help you make dinner? How does following directions help your child do things?

Activity: Set up a small scavenger hunt for your child. Have him follow instructions to get to the end. Discuss how following the clues helped your child reach the goal.

Follow-Up: Use directions to create something together, such as a new toy or craft.

Amelia Bedelia
Author: Peggy Parish
Publisher: HarperCollins Juvenile Books

Amelia Bedelia is a housekeeper who follows her duties *literally*. When told to "dust the house," she takes baby powder and shakes it all over the house. Each item on her to-do list turns into another mistaken idiom and another reason for your child to laugh.

Special Considerations: This is a book that your child should be able to read alone although you may have to help explain some of the idioms.

Learning: Explain to your child the difference between literal and figurative speech. Amelia took everything literally, which caused problems. Explain that sometimes people say things that really mean something else. What is something figurative that you say that could be taken literally? (Getting on my nerves, a piece of cake)

Activity: Write down different idioms. Ask your child to draw what she thinks each means.

Follow-Up: Discuss with your child what each idiom means. Watch a cartoon with your child and see if she can pick out some idioms.

Arthur's Prize Reader

Author: Lillian Hoban
Publisher: Harper Trophy

Arthur is sure he will win the *Super Chimp Comics* contest. He's also sure his sister Violet can't read. But Violet *can* read, maybe even better than Arthur.

Special Considerations: Your child will be challenged by this book, but the words are not too difficult.

Learning: Ask your child if there was ever something he thought he couldn't do, but learned that he *could* do. How did your child feel when he did it?

Activity: Ask your child to draw a picture describing something he thought he couldn't do. Have your child write a sentence or two explaining what he thought he couldn't do and how he felt when he did it. Put it on the refrigerator as a reminder of what your child *can* do.

Follow-Up: Talk with your child about something he wants to do. Set a goal and post it by his picture. When your child reaches the goal, have him change the picture.

Ramona Forever

Author: Beverly Cleary
Publisher: Harper Trophy

Ramona Quimby's life is changing and she can't seem to stay out of trouble. She's eight years old and things just don't seem to be working out right.

Special Considerations: This is one book in a series that follows the life of Ramona Quimby. This is a more difficult chapter book for second graders, but something that your child may relate to and find entertaining.

Learning: This is a great opportunity to discuss your child's life so far. What important things have happened in her life that she thinks would be interesting to read in a book?

Activity: Share with your child some memories of when she was very young, too young to remember. Ask her to think of important times that she does remember and have her write them down. When your child has made a list of things, have her write about them, adding pictures to help explain the stories. Go through your child's stories with her and help her make any corrections that are needed. Make your child's memories into a book.

Follow-Up: Add extra pages to the back of the book. As your child has more important life experiences, you can have her add them and continue the story.

Miss Nelson Is Missing

Author: Harry G. Allard
Publisher: Houghton Mifflin Company

Miss Nelson is a very nice teacher with a class of students who don't treat her very nicely. One day, Miss Nelson doesn't come in, and the students get Ms. Viola Swamp—the ugliest, meanest teacher they've ever met.

Special Considerations: Children will find this a relatively easy book to read, and the ending will catch them by surprise.

Learning: Talk with your child about rules. What rules does he have to follow? What rules do *you* have to follow? Why are rules important?

Activity: Ask your child what he would do if he were Miss Nelson. What would he do to get the class to behave? Ask your child to brainstorm how he would get the class to follow the rules. Help him to rewrite the end of the story and illustrate it.

Follow-Up: Turn your child's ending into a book with a cover and a binding. You can use string through hole-punched paper or straws and string to make the spine, or whatever creative things you can think of.

Ox-Cart Man

Author: Donald Hall
Publisher: Puffin

The book describes the life of a family in the early nineteenth century. It goes through the seasons and years of the family in a New England town.

Special Considerations: This is a simple book with lyrical writing that will be easy for most second graders.

Learning: Explain the differences in seasons, emphasizing how they are different in different areas of the country. Ask your child what similarities and differences there are in the seasons between the New England town in the story and where you live. Do you have changing leaves? Do you have snow in the winter?

Activity: Give your child some magazines to look through and have her cut out and paste pictures that describe the seasons in your area. Have your child explain to you why her pictures are like or unlike those in the book.

Follow-Up: Take a hike in your area to look at things that represent the seasons. If it's fall, check out the changing leaves. If it's spring, look for buds. Is it summer? Observe the temperature and the grown leaves and plants. If it's winter, explain why most animals are not out.

The Three Little Wolves and the Big Bad Pig
Author: Eugene Trivizas
Publisher: Aladdin Library

A twisted version of an old favorite, this story pits three little wolves against one very smart pig. Unlike the original, it has a very happy ending for all.

Learning: Ask your child what materials he thinks were used in the construction of his house. Is it made of sticks? Bricks? Metal? How would your child build a house so strong that it wouldn't be blown over?

Activity: Ask your child to plan and build a house out of materials of his choosing. Let your child explain why he chose the materials and why those materials might make the building stronger.

Follow-Up: Take a drive with your child around your town and look at the architecture. Discuss what the buildings are made of and what makes them strong.

A Chair for My Mother
Author: Vera B. Williams
Publisher: Harper Trophy

Rosa, along with her mother, saves coins in a jar. They want to buy a big, new, comfortable chair for their apartment after losing all of their furniture in a fire.

Special Considerations: This book has some difficult words to read, such as "wonderful" and "comfortable." Your child may need some help.

Learning: Does your child have a money jar or a small collection of change? How much money would she have to save to buy a chair like Rosa's?

Activity: Go through a newspaper or a catalog with your child and find something she would like to buy. How much does it cost? If your child doesn't have a change jar, start one and keep track of how much more your child needs to reach her goal.

Follow-Up: Keep a chart of how much change your child has until the goal is reached.

SOFTWARE FOR SECOND GRADERS

Are you eager to use your computer as a learning tool? I bet you told yourself that educational software is the real reason you needed to get the upgraded media package. Here is the chance to redeem yourself. This appendix provides a list of software titles that are appropriate and interesting for second grade learners. Since your child may be more adept at the technical portion of the activity, it is not listed. If all else fails, refer to the software's user guide. You can find more recommended computer resources for your second grader at www.knowledgeessentials.com.

JumpStart Advanced 2nd Grade
Knowledge Adventure

This product offers a wide variety of math and language arts skills for your child to work on, and it even adds some science, geography, and history into the mix. Children are assigned a guide based on their answers to some questions that assess their learning style. Their big task is to help collect pieces to build a soap shooter and save the day.

Product Focus: Second grade basic skill sets with some science, geography, and history concepts.

Math for Grade 2
School Zone

This product focuses on basic second grade math skills. It is assumed that borrowing and carrying have already been learned, so this could be frustrating to some children. This is a good program for reviewing skills.

Product Focus: Second grade math skills.

Buzz Lightyear 2nd Grade
Disney Interactive

When Woody goes to school with Andy for show-and-tell, the other toys in Andy's room are ready for a day of playing. This product covers in an entertaining way all of the subjects a second grader will learn. The child can move the mouse around the screen and toys will move, indicating an activity.

Product Focus: Second grade basic skill set.

Thinkin' Science
Broderbund

This product covers three levels of science from kindergarten to second grade. It automatically adjusts to the child's level of skill and keeps him or her interested with games and puzzles.

Product Focus: Kindergarten through second grade science concepts and skills.

I Love Spelling!
Global Software Publishing

It's time to practice spelling with this game show–style program. This fun and fast-paced program will help teach five thousand commonly used words in the English language. It is a great way to get a jump on third grade words.

Product Focus: Spelling words and skills.

Smart Steps 2nd Grade
Global Software Publishing

This program encompasses many skills that second graders have or will need to have. It covers reading, math, science, history, and art, combining subjects to use multiple skills. It has three hundred activities to help teach and review basic skills.

Product Focus: Second grade basic skill set.

JumpStart Typing
Knowledge Adventure

Growing up in a computer-based world, children are being expected to learn computer skills earlier. This program teaches basic typing skills, such as correct hand placement and letter combinations. It is one that will grow with your child.

Product Focus: Typing skills and concepts.

I Love the USA
Global Software Publishing

This program is a virtual road trip through the United States. Children can learn about all the different sections of country and about their history, people, and cultures.

Product Focus: Geography and U.S. history skills and information.

Trudy's Time and Place House
Edmark House Series

This program teaches geography, mapping, time-telling, and directions. There are five different activities that will help teach and review concepts, and it has positive feedback to motivate children to succeed.

Product Focus: General second grade skills.

Millie's Math House
Edmark House Series

This product seeks to teach early second graders the math skills they will need further on in their academic career. Using seven main activities and loads of eye-catching graphics, children are motivated to learn about a variety of math topics, including quantities and sequencing.

Product Focus: Second grade basic math skills.

SECOND GRADE TOPICAL CALENDAR

This calendar tells you approximately when the skills covered in this book occur during the school year. There will be variances, of course, but for the most part the skills build on one another, so it is logical that your child will learn things in a certain order.

Reading	Writing	Math	Science and Social Studies
September			
Review skills from first grade	Review skills from first grade	Review skills from first grade	Review skills from first grade
Prefixes and suffixes	Writing sentences	Addition and subtraction	Weather
Vocabulary	Spelling		Local community
October			
Vocabulary	Spelling	Double-digit addition and subtraction	Healthy living
Context clues	Nouns		Types of communities
Parts of a story	Verbs	Shapes	
November			
Vocabulary	Spelling	Place value	The solar system
Comprehension	Nouns	Double-digit addition and subtraction	
Concentration	Verbs		
		Measurement	

Reading	Writing	Math	Science and Social Studies
December			
Vocabulary	Pronouns	Double-digit addition and subtraction	Earth rotation and tilt
Parts of a story	Spelling		Seasons
		Measurement	Weather
		Shapes	Community
January			
Vocabulary	Spelling	Double-digit addition and subtraction	Government
Context clues	Adverbs		Weather
Sequencing		Place value	Earth rotation
Parts of a story		Estimating	Other planets' rotations
Plot			
February			
Vocabulary	Spelling	Double-digit addition and subtraction with borrowing	Government
Context cues	Adjectives		Map skills
Setting		Place value	
		Estimating	
March			
Vocabulary	Spelling	Double-digit addition and subtraction with borrowing	Government
Characters—main and other	Nouns, verbs, pronouns, adjectives, adverbs	Place value	Map skills
			Living things—plants and animals
April			
Vocabulary	Spelling	Extended operations	Weather and seasons
Parts of a story	Nouns, verbs, pronouns, adjectives, adverbs	Measurement	Living things—plants and animals
Extended concentration			
May			
Vocabulary	Spelling	Extended operations	Map skills
Parts of a story	Nouns, verbs, pronouns, adjectives, adverbs	Measurement	Healthy living
Extended concentration			

GLOSSARY

accountability   Holding students responsible for what they learn and teachers responsible for what they teach.

achievement test   A test designed to efficiently measure the amount of knowledge and/or skill a person has acquired. This helps evaluate student learning in comparison with a standard or norm.

assessment   Measuring a student's learning.

authentic assessment   The concept of model, practice, and feedback in which students know what excellent performance is and are guided to practice an entire concept rather than bits and pieces in preparation for eventual understanding.

benchmark   A standard by which student performance can be measured in order to compare it with and improve one's own skills or learning.

Bloom's taxonomy   A classification system for learning objectives that consists of six levels ranging from knowledge (which focuses on the reproduction of facts) to evaluation (which represents higher-level thinking).

competency test   A test intended to determine whether a student has met established minimum standards of skills and knowledge and is thus eligible for promotion, graduation, certification, or other official acknowledgment of achievement.

concept   An abstract, general notion—a heading that characterizes a set of behaviors and beliefs.

content goals   Statements that are like learning standards or learning objectives, but which only describe the topics to be studied, not the skills to be performed.

criterion-referenced test   A test in which the results can be used to determine a student's progress toward mastery of a content area or designated objectives of an instructional program. Performance is compared to an expected level of mastery in a content area rather than to other students' scores.

curriculum   The content and skills that are taught at each grade level.

curriculum alignment   The connection of subjects across grade levels, cumulatively, to build comprehensive, increasingly complex instructional programs.

high-stakes testing   Any testing program whose results have important consequences for students, teachers, colleges, and/or areas, such as promotion, certification, graduation, or denial/approval of services and opportunity.

IQ test   A psychometric test that scores the performance of certain intellectual tasks and can provide assessors with a measurement of general intelligence.

learning objectives   A set of expectations that are needed to meet the learning standard.

learning standards   Broad statements that describe what content a student should know and what skills a student should be able to demonstrate in different subject areas.

measurement   Quantitative description of student learning and qualitative description of student attitude.

median   The point on a scale that divides a group into two equal subgroups. The median is not affected by low or high scores as is the mean. (See also **norm**.)

metacognition   The knowledge of one's own thinking processes and strategies, and the ability to consciously reflect and act on the knowledge of cognition to modify those processes and strategies.

multiple-choice test   A test in which students are presented with a question or an incomplete sentence or idea. The students are expected to choose the correct or best answer or completion from a menu of alternatives.

norm   A distribution of scores obtained from a norm group. The norm is the midpoint (or median) of scores or performance of the students in that group. Fifty percent will score above the norm and 50 percent will score below it.

norm group   A random group of students selected by a test developer to take a test to provide a range of scores and establish the percentiles of performance for use in determining scoring standards.

norm-referenced test   A test in which a student or a group's performance is compared to that of a norm group. The results are relative to the performance of an external group and are designed to be compared with the norm group, resulting in a performance standard. These tests are often used to measure and compare students, schools, districts, and states on the basis of norm-established scales of achievement.

outcome   An operationally defined educational goal, usually a culminating activity, product, or performance that can be measured.

performance-based assessment   Direct observation and rating of student performance of an educational objective, often an ongoing observation over a period of time, and typically involving the creation of products dealing with real life. Performance-based assessments use performance criteria to determine the degree to which a student has met an achievement target. Important elements of performance-based assessment include clear goals or performance criteria clearly articulated and communicated to the learner.

performance goals   Statements that are like learning standards or learning objectives, but they only describe the skills to be performed, not the content to be studied.

portfolio assessment   A systematic and organized collection of a student's work that exhibits to others the direct evidence of a student's efforts, achievements, and progress over a period of time. The collection should involve the student in selection of its contents and should include information about the performance criteria, the rubric or criteria for judging merit, and evidence of student self-relocation or evaluation. It should include representative work, providing documentation of the learner's performance and a basis for evaluation of the student's progress. Portfolios may include a variety of demonstrations of learning.

BIBLIOGRAPHY

Bloom, B. S. (ed.) (1956). *Taxonomy of Educational Objectives: The Classification of Educational Goals: Handbook I, Cognitive Domain.* New York: Longmans, Green.

Brainerd, C. J. (1978). *Piaget's Theory of Intelligence.* New Jersey: Prentice Hall, Inc.

Evans, R. (1973). *Jean Piaget: The Man and His Ideas.* New York: E. P. Dutton & Co., Inc.

Lavatelli, C. (1973). *Piaget's Theory Applied to an Early Childhood Curriculum.* Boston: American Science and Engineering, Inc.

London, C. (1988). "A Piagetian Constructivist Perspective on Curriculum Development." *Reading Improvement 27*, 82–95.

Piaget, J. (1972). "Development and Learning." In Lavatelli, C. S., and Stendler, F. *Reading in Child Behavior and Development.* New York: Harcourt Brace Janovich.

———— (1972). *To Understand Is to Invent.* New York: The Viking Press, Inc.

Shure, M. B. (1993). *Interpersonal Problem Solving and Prevention: A Comprehensive Report of Research and Training.* A five-year longitudinal study, Kindergarten through grade 4, no. MH-40801. Washington, D.C.: National Institute of Mental Health.

Shure, M. B., and G. Spivack (1980). "Interpersonal Problem Solving as a Mediator of Behavioral Adjustment in Preschool and Kindergarten Children." *Journal of Applied Developmental Psychology 1*, 29–44.

——— (1982). "Interpersonal Problem-Solving in Young Children: A Cognitive Approach to Prevention." *American Journal of Community Psychology 10*, 341–356.

Sigel, I., and R. Cocking (1977). *Cognitive Development from Childhood to Adolescence: A Constructivist Perspective.* New York: Holt, Rinehart and Winston.

Singer, D., and T. Revenson (1978). *A Piaget Primer: How a Child Thinks.* New York: International Universities Press, Inc.

Willis, Mariaemma, and Victoria Hodson (1999). *Discover Your Child's Learning Style.* New York: Crown Publishing Group.

INDEX

accommodation, of information, 14

accountability, 32, 185–186

Addition Bingo (math activity), 106

analysis, in cognitive learning taxonomy, 25, 27

And the Moral of the Story Is . . . (reading activity), 55–56

anxieties, about third grade, 200

application, in cognitive learning taxonomy, 25, 27

assimilation, of information, 14

attention span, 18

auditory learning style, 21–23

Aye or Nay (social studies activity), 160–161

Basketball (reading activity), 50–51

Bird's–Eye View (social studies activity), 168–169

Bloom, Benjamin, 24–29

Body Map (science activity), 133–134

Calisthenics (science activity), 131–133

City Mouse, Country Mouse (social studies activity), 152–153

Closer Constellations (science activity), 136–137

cognitive development
  Piaget on, 13–16
  readiness for third grade in, 199–200
  teaching thinking skills, 173–179

cognitive learning levels, 24–29

Come See Where I Live! (social studies activity), 154

Comic Strip Mix–Up (reading activity), 54–55

communication
  with teachers, 6–8
  for teaching thinking skills, 173–175

communities, in social studies, 151–158

comprehension, 176–177
  in cognitive learning taxonomy, 25, 26
  in reading, 37–38, 52–63

concentration, 52–53, 176

concrete operational stage, of cognitive development, 14–15

control issues, 188–191

conversations, 2

Creepy Books (writing activity), 79–80

Cross (math activity), 104–105

decoding, in reading, 37–38

Definition Cereal Words (reading activity), 49–50

development, child's, 2, 10, 18

developmental goals, 15–19

developmental stages, 13–16, 24

Dice–y Writing (writing activity), 78–79